END OF THE PATRIARCHY

Gerhard Falk

University Press of America,® Inc.
Lanham · Boulder · New York · Toronto · Plymouth, UK

**Copyright © 2016 by
University Press of America,® Inc.**
4501 Forbes Boulevard
Suite 200
Lanham, Maryland 20706
UPA Acquisitions Department (301) 459-3366

Unit A, Whitacre Mews, 26-34 Stannary Street,
London SE11 4AB, United Kingdom

Library of Congress Control Number: 2015954400
ISBN: 978-0-7618-6706-7 (clothbound : alk. paper)
eISBN: 978-0-7618-6707-4

Dedication

This book is dedicated to my wife, Ursula, who has shown me all these years what love really means.

Table of Contents

Preface

A Survey of American Men

In 2010, Esquire Magazine conducted a survey of American men. According to that survey, assembled by a professional surveying organization, there were more twenty-year-old men in the United States in 2010 than any other age group. The second largest age group was men aged fifty. These two groups, age twenty and fifty, answered the same questions, with the result that a considerable difference in beliefs and attitudes was uncovered by this survey.

Sixty-one percent of the 20-year-old men interviewed claimed to be happy, compared with just 49% among men aged fifty. Forty-one percent of twenty-year-olds voted that the best role model for young American men is Barack Obama. Thirty-two percent of fifty-year-old men agreed with that estimate.[1]

Over half, I.e. 57%, of twenty-year-old men played video games daily and 24% played such games every other day. Thus, eighty-one percent of adult men in that age cohort play such games, while 53% of fifty-year-olds do the same.

Forty-one percent of fifty-year-olds and 36% of twenty-year-old men consider the best job in the United States to be an A-list movie star. This leaves President of the United States far behind, at eleven percent and twenty percent respectively.[2]

It is by no means surprising that about one half of all men in both age groups get most of their news from television, and that only nine percent of twenty-year-olds and eleven percent of fifty-year-olds learn about the news from newspapers.

Among twenty-year-old men, 29% answered that they had been involved in a physical altercation during the year past. Only 5% of fifty-year-old men had such an experience.

Both twenty-year-olds and fifty-year-olds favored football over all other sports as their favorite spectator sport, with basketball and baseball tied for second place. The exception is that 26% of twenty-year-olds viewed ultimate fighting as a favorite, which only 7% of fifty-year-olds favored.

Drinking alcohol is as much an occupation of twenty-year-olds as fifty-year-olds. Thirteen to fifteen percent of both groups agreed that they had five of more drinks in a single sitting two to three days ago and eight percent of both groups drank that much one week ago. Forty-four percent of twenty-year-olds and twenty percent of fifty-year-olds answered "never."[3]

Nearly half, or 46%, of twenty-year-olds exercise only occasionally, if at all. Fifty-three percent of 50-year-olds agree. Those who find exercise very important are far more likely to consider themselves happy than those who do not exercise.

Sixty-nine percent of twenty-year-olds claimed that they believed "in God." Fourteen percent did not believe this. Eighty percent of fifty-year-olds believed or said they believed, while nine percent did not believe in God.

Despite the availability of Twitter, Facebook, email, texting, and the telephone, thirty-one percent of 20-year-old men and fifty percent of fifty-year-old men prefer to communicate with others in person.

The vast majority of twenty-year-olds as well as fifty-year-old men believe that a wife should decide for herself whether or not she seeks to work outside the home or stay at home or work part time. Their answer to a question about this overwhelmingly asserts: "Whatever she wants".[4]

A truly astonishing answer was given by 36% of 50-year-old men, who claimed to have had more that fifteen sexual partners. Only 5% of fifty-year-olds claimed to have had 13 sexual partners. Only 8% of twenty-year-old men made such a claim, inasmuch as their young age would preclude such achievement, ipso facto.

The survey next asked both twenty-year-old and 50-year-old men to state their income. Fifty-three percent of twenty-year-olds revealed earnings of less than $25,000. Among 50-year-old men, 53% earned between $25,000 and $50,000, eleven percent earned between $75,000 and $100,000, and 7% earned $101,000 to $150,000. Two percent in both categories earned more than $150,000 annually.

Politically, forty-three percent of twenty-year-old men and thirty-three percent of fifty-year-old men are Independents, favoring neither Democrats nor Republicans. As to same sex marriage, 54% of twenty-year-olds favor this arrangement, while 54% of fifty-year-olds are opposed.

Securing the border is viewed as the best means of insuring immigration reform, according to thirty-three percent of tsenty-year-old men and 50% of fifty-year-old men.

Given a choice to select as the most worrisome condition facing the American people, both groups of men chose unemployment or the economy as the most worrisome. The other choices were the environment terrorism, the federal deficit and impotency.

This survey of the attitudes of American men allows us a minimum view of male beliefs and considerations affecting elections and the manner in which men view themselves.

In 2015 American men are gradually being reduced to followers of American women. For centuries men dominated and women followed; the opposite is already true for many American men. For example, the National Center for Policy Analysis reported in 2014 that 10.4 million American men between the ages of 25 and 54 years are unemployed. These are the years in which adults are most productive and earn most of their lifetime incomes.

Looking back to 1970, the Wall Street Journal discovered that then six percent of American men age 20–54 were not working. By 2007, thirteen percent in that age group were out of work. That number rose to twenty percent in 2009 and then fell to 17 percent by December 2013. Because two thirds of these men were not looking for work, they were not counted among the unemployed by government statisticians. These men have given up looking for employment, as 40 percent have been unemployed for at least six months. This came about because many men who were once employed in unskilled factory work no longer have marketable skills. Their erstwhile jobs have been "outsourced" and sent to India or China or are being done by robots.

Another consequence of this unrecognized unemployment is the rise of disability benefits delivered to these men. In 1980, only 3 percent of men between the ages of 25 and 64 collected disability benefits. In 2013 that number rose to 5.5%. Over 2 million of those men were less than 55 years old. It is a matter of record that very few of those who ever received disability benefits have ever returned to work. This is also true of those whose application for disability benefits have been rejected.

This, then, is a picture of the "patriarchy" as it exists at the beginning of its end. That end is now certain, as the rise of women in the 21st century has already demonstrated.[5]

Notes

1. No author, "20/50: The Esquire Survey of American Men," *Esquire Magazine,* vol. 17, no.1 (October, 2013):1.

2. Ibid.:2

3. Ibid.:4

4. Ibid:15

5. Mark Peters and David Wessel, "More Men in Prime Working age Don't Have Jobs," *The Wall Street Journal.* (February 6, 2014):1.

Acknowledgments

I am indebted to my son Clifford Falk for his help in formatting and proofreading this manuscript, and to Dr. Ursula Falk, my wife and life companion, for all the support she has given me these many years.

Chapter One

Women and the American Economy

I

For centuries past, men have earned more than their wives if married women worked outside the home. Such outside work by wives was indeed unusual and even condemned in the Victorian age. Today, in the 21st century, a major shift in the relations between the genders has occurred in America. This is the ascendancy of women in economics, education, family, religion, government, and communication. Indeed, the gender revolution which this ascendancy represents is not complete. In 2015 the average income of working women is still less than that of American men. The majority of clergy and the majority of government officials are still men. However, the education of women has already exceeded that of American men, so that female domination in all areas of American leadership positions is now inevitable.

This is illustrated by the fact that in 21st century America, more and more married women earn more than their husbands, as illustrated by statistics furnished by the U.S. Bureau of Labor Statistics.

This trend was already visible in the 1970's and reached 24 percent in 1987 among wives whose husbands were out of work. That number increased to 38% in 2012.

Among those who were both working, nearly 18% of wives earned more than their husbands in 1987, a number which rose to 29% in 2012.[1]

A study by the Pew Research Center published in May 2013 showed that women were then "leading breadwinners in forty percent of American households."

In 1960, only four percent of American wives earned more than their husbands. According to the Pew study, that number rose to 24% in 2013. Of those earning more than their husbands, 49% have a college degree, sixty-five percent are white, and 67 percent are between the ages of thirty and fifty. Despite the evidence that more women are better educated than their spouses, most women still earn less than their men.[2]

Nevertheless, four in ten American households with children under age eighteen now include a mother who is either the only or primary earner in her family, a number which has quadrupled since 1960. These changes came about as it became more and more acceptable for women to join the workforce. Moreover, it has become commonplace to find single mothers who raise children, as two thirds of mothers who are the chief support of their family are single. This need to rely on the earnings of women has been augmented and increased by those who are married to construction workers and those men in manufacturing who lost their jobs during the recession beginning in 2008, which also included massive layoffs in the public sector. Women who at one time claimed that they prefer to stay home rather than go to work were about twenty percent of the married population. That number has now (2014) risen to 34 percent. The median annual income for these women, many of whom are Hispanic, is $23,000. However, the median annual income for women with a college education, primarily of European descent, is $80,000.[3]

Public opinion in this regard has changed dramatically over the years, as only 28% of those surveyed by Pew agree that it is better for a husband to out-earn a wife. Yet, it has also been discovered that women who are not working but are most likely to earn more than their husbands will often stay out of the workforce for fear of provoking a divorce. Among those couples married in 2011 and later, thirty percent included women earning more than their husbands.[4]

In 1960, only four percent of single mothers were never married. In 2014, this has risen to 45 percent.

Dual earning couples are now commonplace, as 78% of workers are married to working spouses, of whom 75% work full time.[5]

Brennen, Barnett and Gareis published a longitudinal study of couples whose female partner earns more than the male partner. This resulted in finding that the economic independence of women has led to a decline in their desire to marry or remain married. Other studies support this view, as Heckert, et. al. found that the greater the dependence of the wife on her husband's financial support, the lower the chances of marital dissolution.[6]

That marital dissolution may also be related to the decline in husbands' self esteem, as their wives' income increases or exceeds theirs. Many such husbands feel rising competition with their high earning wives, as the "good provider" role is important to men but not that central to women.[7]

A number of surveys have shown that husbands are as much supportive of egalitarian treatment relative to wages and other issues as are wives. In fact, one study showed that one third of husbands were more egalitarian than their wives. However, the majority, I.e. two thirds of husbands, were more likely to approve of the egalitarian model when wives were the junior partner in the earning area. Among couples in which the wife earned more than the husband, the wife earns about 59% of total income.[8]

In view of the ever greater number of women who earn more than men, it is not surprising that some of this increase in income is the product of education and therefore the ascendancy of women into management positions.

While this has been true since the 1970's, there remains a gender gap with reference to management, which may well be eliminated in the next decade but is most visible in the second decade of the 21st century. It is evident that female graduates of highly ranked MBA (Master of Business Administration) programs take lower ranking jobs than do men with the same background. This means that women of equal education and experience earn less than men and therefore also have less formal authority than men.[9]

The reasons for this gender gap are traditionally that fewer women than men have had the educational background needed for top management jobs, that women have preferred different types of jobs than men, and that women have generally acquired less of the work experience accumulated by men.

Nevertheless, since 1970, when only 13 percent of management jobs in American business and industry were held by women, in 1998 forty-six percent of managers were women, and in 2010 this number declined to 41 percent, even as women's share in the private sector has risen to 47 percent.

This temporary decline is also visible in the proportion of women among top executives. In 1970, twelve percent of CEO's were women, and in 1991 this figure rose to 39 percent. Yet, by 2010, only 28 percent of top executives were women, as the largest firms have the fewest female executives.[10]

One measure of success in the business world is inclusion in the so-called "Fortune 500," a list of the highest earning corporations in the United States. According to that list published annually by Fortune Magazine, there were no women CEO's on that list in 1995, the first year of publication. In 2010, eleven Fortune 500 corporations had women CEOs, constituting only 2.5% of all such appointments. Yet, in May of 2014, the 49 women then listed as CEO's of American companies constituted 4.8% of Fortune 1000 positions.[11]

In part, the achievements of women in the business world are due to their ever increasing education, which has outpaced men over the years since 1970, when women earned 43% of the bachelor's degrees and less than 3 percent had advanced degrees. In 2011 and later, women have earned 57 percent of bachelor's degrees, sixty percent of master's, and 52% of doctor's degrees.[12]

Many women and men differ in their job preferences. Women are evidently more concerned with the wellbeing of others than is true of men, and are less interested in material benefits and competition than is true of men. The latter is of course the value held most important in corporate America. Women also have a different view of finding purpose and meaning in life than is the case among men.

Beutel and Martini, in a study of "human capital," found that men value job security and promotion opportunities more than women, while women value a sense of accomplishment more than men.[13]

The differences in female and male job preferences are probably not related to sex but to the status-role of women and men. This means that women are less likely to hold top positions in industry and business than is true of men and that therefore they place less value on their careers.

Work experience is also related to gender in this country. In the 1970's, only 41 percent of women were in the labor force, but by 2009 fifty-four percent of women and 65 percent of men were in the labor force. Sixty-one percent of married women and 64 percent of single women were in the labor force in 2009 alongside 65 percent of American men. Evidently, women had equaled their labor force participation with men in that year.[14]

Women are obliged to take more time out of their careers than men in order to tend to children. This feature of female life directly impacts their work experience relative to men. Gaps between men's and women's work experience increases with age. Thus median job tenure for men age 50–64 is 10.1 years. For women in the same cohort the median job tenure is 7.00 years. [15]

Cultural factors related to beliefs concerning the roles women and men are also influential in the ascendancy of women in the 21st century. Traditionally it was the role of women to be followers and helpers of men. Women were not viewed as leaders or self-promoters in the world of business or the professions. Included in these beliefs was the prejudice to the effect that men are good at mathematics and that mathematics were not for women. These beliefs were widely held, taught in schools, and also became the opinion of most women who demeaned themselves by accepting as "truth" these stereotypes.

In the 21st century this view has been defeated by women who have achieved degrees in mathematics, engineering, physics, computer science, and other areas based on mathematical principles.

Since capacity in science and engineering has led to upper management jobs, the beliefs about female incompetence in these areas have for years blocked female advancement in business and industry. With the defeat of these beliefs, more and more women are achieving higher levels of employment, including chief executive officers of some of America's most important corporations. [16]

The effort of women regarding promotion to executive status in the world of business and industry is affected by the needs of children. This is an area which cannot be ignored and with which mothers must contend no matter what their work ambitions may be. According to several public opinion polls, almost all Americans accept that married women without children have a right to work full time. However, only 11 percent of those polled agree that women with young children should work full time, 34% approve of women with young children working part time, and 56% wish such mothers could not work at all. [17] Working women are handicapped by the traditional expectation that they do the housework for the family. Therefore working women fulfill their gender role by doing two jobs, including all that child care and domestic labor imply. These expectations have persisted despite the increase in the number of women in the labor force. Indeed many men, married to working wives, have assumed the tasks of some housework. Nevertheless it has been estimated that female managers work sixty hours or more each week. [18]

Among the high achieving women who have reached executive positions, there are many who have left management jobs and who have since then stayed home with their children. Evidently, some mothers find it difficult to leave children to babysitters, nannies, boarding schools, and pre-schools. Pressure to stay with children is not only located within the mother, but is also the product of the media, who excoriate mothers who leave their children for work. [19]

One result of these pressures is that a good number of women in management jobs forego marriage and children lest they cannot compete with men. The corporate culture demands that devotion to the job must come before any other considerations. Some women attempt to have it both ways and therefore work part time, a maneuver which is characterized as lack of devotion to the job.[20]

Powerful stereotypes associate management roles with men and not with women. Commonly, when people think manager, they think man, not woman. Therefore, managers are expected to do things typically associated with masculinity, such as imposing their wishes on subordinates, acting assertively, and standing out from the group. Self-confidence, aggression, and ambition are further characteristics of men, not usually associated with women. Women are more likely to have democratic, participatory, and collaborative methods of management than is true of men. Because American culture has for so long stereotyped women as incapable of leadership, many women have adopted this view of themselves and acted accordingly. It is therefore the task of women executives to challenge these beliefs, to alter the stereotype, and to pursue management roles in a feminist fashion without attempting to impersonate male behavior.[21]

II

During the fifteen years ending in 2012, the number of women owned businesses grew by 54%, so that there are now at least 8.3 million women-owned businesses in the United States. Women owned businesses employ 7.7 million people. That is more than the three largest American employers, McDonalds, IBM, and Wal-Mart combined. These women-owned businesses generate approximately $1.23 billion a year. This means that there has been a 15% increase in women-owned business revenue in the past 15 years. The industries with the highest concentration of women are educational services, health care and social assistance, and entertainment.

Arizona, Nevada, Wyoming and North Dakota are the top states for women-owned businesses. The top cities in this respect ae Sacramento, California; San Antonio and Houston, Texas, as well as Baltimore and Washington, D.C.

Two percent of women-owned businesses bring in one million dollars or more in annual revenue. This is true of 5% of all businesses. [22]

There is a National Association of Women Business Owners who claim that there are ten million women owned businesses across the country, located in every county of the union. Founded in 1975, the Association has chapters in every county in the country. 34% of NAWBO members earn more than $500,000. Fifty-eight percent of NAWBO members access capital though credit cards. Another 37 percent use private and family savings to finance their businesses.[23]

III

Although only 4.8% of chief executive officers of America's largest corporations were women as of 2013, the female contingent of chief executives includes some of the largest companies in the world. The following examples of the most successful female CEO's is not typical of employed American women any more than such a list would be typical of the average male employee. It does nevertheless indicate the degree to which new opportunities for American women have promoted some to the highest levels of American industry. This means that numerous women not included among the most successful have attained a considerable financial success in recent years. This predicts that the male oligarchy is over and that at least gender equality, if not female superiority, will be the inevitable outcome of the present trend in women's challenge to the ancient patriarchy.

Examples of some of the most prominent women in business, industry and the professions are here presented.

Mary T. Barra is president of General Motors, a company which employs 212,000 people. An electrical engineer, she also holds the degree of Master of Business Administration. Her compensation is $16.2 million annually. Her father was a tool and die maker at GM and she has been employed by GM for 33 years. She began her career at GM in 1980 as a co-op student at Kettering University and the Pontiac Motor Division. She graduated with a Bachelor of Science Degree in Electrical Engineering and subsequently received a fellowship from GM, leading to a Master of Business Administration from Stanford University.

She is married to Tony Barra, who has a similar education and is president of a consulting firm. They have two children.[24]

Marissa Mayer is president of Yahoo, where she is paid $36.6 million a year. Mayer is a graduate of Stanford University, where she earned a bachelor's degree in symbolic systems and a master's degree in artificial intelligence. She worked for Google at its beginning, when it had only 19 employees, and was appointed CEO of Yahoo in June Of 2012. Ranked "No. 1" by Fortune Magazine among "under forty" executives, her wealth is estimated at $300 million. She married Zach Bogue, a wealthy investment lawyer and partner in a venture capital firm. They bought a mansion in San Francisco for $35 million.

Irene Rosenfeld is CEO of Mondelez International, formerly known as Kraft, with a salary of $28.8 million.

A native of New York, Rosenfeld earned a B.A. in Psychology and an M.A. in Business and a Ph.D. in Statistics and Marketing from Cornell University.

For thirty years, Rosenfeld has worked in the food and beverage industry. This led to her appointment in 2004 as Chair and CEO of Frito-Lay, a division of Pepsico. Two years later, in 2006, she was appointed Chief Executive Officer at Kraft Foods, where she was credited with achieving major success in Russia,

Canada, and the United States for the company. Her income in 2010 was $13,994,780, making her 48th on the Forbes list of executive pay.

In 2011, Rosenfeld was appointed CEO of the newly named Mondelez International, Inc., a $31 billion corporation selling food all over the world.

Irene Rosenfeld is the widow of Richard Rosenfeld, with whom she had two daughters. Her second husband is Richard Illgen, an investment banker.[25]

Margaret Whitman is the president of Hewlett-Packard Co. She was appointed in 2011, earning $1 million a year. In 2013, her salary was raised to $1.5 million. Hewlett-Packard achieved a profit of $5 billion on revenues of $112 billion in 2013. Hewlett-Packard had experienced a revenue decline of 12% before Whitman became CEO.

Whitman accepted the rather low salary in 2011 because she is a billionaire. Her wealth is estimated at $1.9 billion. Furthermore, Whitman was granted a stock package worth $16.5 million.[26]

Prior to becoming CEO at Hewlett-Packard, Whitman was Chief Executive Officer at eBay, an online store. In that position Whitman was the first woman to become a billionaire.

Whitman was born into a wealthy Boston family. She graduated from Princeton University in 1977 and later earned an M.B.A. degree from Harvard University. She was then hired by Proctor and Gamble in Ohio. She married medial student Griffin Harsh IV and relocated to San Francisco, where Harsh entered he practice of neurosurgery. She had one child and then worked for Disney. In 2010, Whitman ran for governor of California, but lost to Jerry Brown despite having spent $160 million on her campaign. She then held several administrative positions in a number of different industries when she was offered the position of CEO at eBay. In 2011, she was appointed President and CEO of Hewlett-Packard.

Safra Catz is the president of Oracle, a computer technology corporation. Her annual income is $51.7 million. The corporation earned $4.13 billion in one year. Catz is the oldest child of Leonard Catz, professor of physics at the University of Massachusetts. Her mother Judith was born in the Ukraine and survived the Holocaust. Safra Catz is a graduate of the Wharton School of Business at the University of Pennsylvania and the Harvard University School of Law. Her husband, Gal Tirosh, is a soccer coach in Palo Alto, California. He does not earn fifty million dollars a year.

Sharen Jester Turney is the President of Victoria's Secret, a ladies apparel business. The company has annual sales of $1.2 billion sold in stores nationwide. Ms. Turney earns $25,620,000 a year. She owns three homes in New Albany, Ohio, New York City, and Florida.

She is a graduate of the school of business of the University of Oklahoma. She began her career at Foley's department stores and later worked for Federal Department Stores and Neiman-Marcus, a Dallas, Texas based department store.

Her husband, Charles Turney, is an accountant who stays at home with their one child, a son, Matthew.

In October 2011, Virginia Rometty became the first female president of IBM (International Business Machines) in the 100 year old history of that company, where she has worked for more than thirty years. In October 2012, she also assumed the role of chairman of IBM. The company attains $20 billon in revenue. Her salary is $16.2 million.

Rometty is a native of Chicago. She graduated from Northwestern University with a degree in electrical engineering. Her first job was with General Motors in Detroit. There she met her husband Mark Rometty. They have no children. In 1981, she joined IBM as a systems engineer in the Detroit office. From there she accepted several assignments and then became group executive for sales marketing in 2009.

Rometty is a member of numerous boards of directors of charitable and educational foundations, such as the Columbia Business School.[27]

Mary Jackson Sammons if the president and CEO of Rite Aid, earning a salary of $2.9 million. She earned a B.A. degree from Marylhurst College in 1970 and then joined Fred Meyer Stores as a trainee in 1979. She rose from one assignment to another until she became president in 1998. The next year she was appointed president of Rite Aid and Chief Executive Officer in 2000. Rite Aid has 73,000 employees.

She assumed the CEO position at Rite Aid at a time when that company appeared to be in serious financial trouble. It seemed that the company was about to face bankruptcy. However, Sammons returned the company to profitability. She was cited by Chain Drug Review for "engineering one of the remarkable recoveries in chain drug history." She acquired the Eckard and Brooks drug store chains, resulting in Rite Aid including 6,100 stores in its nationwide chain.

She is married to Nickolas F. Sammons, with whom she has one child.

The chair of Annaly Capital Management, a real estate investment trust, is Welllington Denahan Norris. She is paid $28.5 million. Jane Ellers, president of Children's Place, which sells clothing for children, earns $17.2 million, and the CEO of Pepsi Cola, Indra Nooyi, earns $14.2 million. Sherilyn McCoy earns $12.9 million as president of Avon Products. Debra Cafaro is president of Ventas, a real estate investment trust, earning $11.2 million. Wai Bing To of Hong Kong Television Productions was compensated at a rate of $3,116,000 per year as of 2013.[28]

Ursula Burns is the chair and CEO of the Xerox Corporation, earning $5.5 million annual salary. Burns is a graduate of the Polytechnic Institute of New York University, where she earned a degree in mechanical engineering. She also holds a master's degree in mechanical engineering from Columbia University. She has been an employee of Xerox since 1980. She was appointed executive assistant to the chairman of Xerox, Paul Allaire, from 1992 to 2000. In 2000 she was promoted to senior vice president of corporate strategic services in charge of manufacturing and supply chain operations. Thereafter she was in charge of Xerox global research and product development.

When Ann Mulcahy became CEO of Xerox, Burns became her assistant until Mulcahy left in 2009 when Burns became CEO and Chairwoman two years later.

Burns is married to Lloyd Bean who retired from Xerox. She has two children.

IV

A considerable number of women have entered the health delivery field. The majority are nurses, although some have succeeded in hospital management.

According to the Bureau of Labor Statistics, there were 934,000 physicians practicing in the United States in 2013. 35.5% of these, or 327,000, were women with an average annual income of $144,810. Male physicians earned $168,000 a year.[29]

"Hospital Review" has listed 52 women involved in hospital management who are regarded as "healthcare leaders." Only six of these administrators are listed as M.D.'s. A few have nursing degrees. The majority have degrees in hospital administration or business.

Featured as a prime example of female success was Marna Bergstrom, the president and CEO of Yale-New Haven Hospital. The first woman to chair that organization, she reputedly earns an annual salary of $2,022,541. She began her career at that hospital in 1979 as an administrative "fellow."

Elizabeth G. Nabel, M.D. is one of the few physicians to head a hospital. She is CEO of Brigham and Women's Hospital in Boston, where she is paid $1.94 million yearly. Nabel is a member of a large number of prestigious associations and has been awarded numerous prizes and recognitions. It is therefore evident that she is a medical politician, as are others who have learned to benefit from charitable contributions.

A prime example of the immense incomes pocketed by hospital administrators is Ora Hirsch Pescovitz, recently resigned from the University of Michigan Health Center hospital. There she collected $885,000 a year. Undoubtedly the oversight of a large health system has to be well compensated. We are reminded, however, that the President of the United States earns less than half of the salary paid this hospital administrator.[30]

Similar and even greater incomes are allocated to chief executive officers of so-called charities. Although a charity is normally understood to be a means of helping those who cannot help themselves, it is now evident that "charities" are in fact payrolls for those who know how to manipulate the charity system in their favor. Accordingly, salaries of $1 million or more are not uncommon among the chief executive officers of American charities. It needs to be remembered that every CEO has numerous assistants who also benefit from contributions made to charities by those who seek to help the poor.

Included in the list of major beneficiaries of the charity dollar is Caryl Stern, the CEO of the United Nations Children's Fund. She collects $454,857 per year. Then there is Marcia Evans, former President of the Red Cross. She took home $651,957 plus expenses. After her resignation, Gail McGovern was appointed at a salary of $565,000.[31]

Nancy Brinker is the chair of The Breast Cancer Foundation. This allows her to "earn" $684,000, a salary so high that a number of former donors have failed to contribute any further.[32]

In 2010, the Boys & Girls Clubs of America were closing a number of their clubs around the country. In that year, the CEO of this charity, Roxanne Spillett, was "raking in" $988,581, according to an I.R.S. filing. Because this charity receives millions of dollars in taxpayers' money, Senators Grassley, Tom Coburn, Jon Kyl, and John Cornyn sent a letter of the chairman of the board of Boys and Girls Clubs questioning whether to allocate any further tax dollars to that organization. Evidently, this "charity" and so many others have become "rackets," in the sense that a "racket" is defined as a means of making money without rendering anything in return. It is once more important to remember that the President of the United States presides over 320 million Americans for only $400,000 a year.[33]

V

In 2012, 21,043 American women were awarded a law degree. This constituted 47.3% of all graduates. As the proportion of women law students increased, the number of women employed in the law increased as well, so that the percentage of female lawyers rose to one third of the 329,000 American lawyers.

Twenty percent of editors-in-chief of the fifty most prestigious law reviews are women, and women were 20 percent of law school deans in 2010.

Women are well represented in the judiciary, as fifty-one percent of judicial clerks are women. This includes federal, state, and local judges. Three Supreme Court judges out of nine are women and 31% of judges on the courts of appeal are women, as are 24.1% of federal court judges. Twenty-seven percent of state court judges are women.[34]

The weekly salaries of women lawyers lagged behind that of men in 2013. Male lawyers earned an average of $1,884 per week and women received a weekly income of $1,631, or 86.6% of male salaries.[35]

Five women have been presidents of the American Bar Association. Roberta Cooper Ramo (1990–1996); Martha W. Barnett (2000–2001), Karen J. Mathis, (2000–2007), Carolyn B. Lamm (2000–2010), and Laurel Bellows, (2010–2013).[36]

Among lawyers working for corporations, 22% are women, although only four of the country's largest corporations have women in top legal positions. These are Wal-Mart, Honeywell, United States Steel, FedEx, and Lockheed-Martin. The number of female partners in American law firms is only nineteen percent. One of these is Mary Ann Iantorno Hynes. She is senior counsel at Dentons, an international law firm with headquarters in Chicago, where her compensation exceeds a million dollars.

A graduate of Loyola University, she earned a law degree from the John Marshall Law School, an LLM degree, and an MBA degree from Lake Forest University.

Her husband, James Hynes, is a lawyer in the village of Niles, Illinois, where he also serves as a village trustee. They have two children and a number of grandchildren.

Other female lawyers who have attained high paying appointments at major American corporations are Katherine Adams at Honeywell, Susan Folsom at U.S. Steel, Mary Jones at Deere Co., and Ivonne Carbera at Bristol-Myers.

VI

Heretofore the word "inventor" has invariably meant a male. This view overlooks that women have been responsible for a number of inventions, some of which were produced in the nineteenth century. Josephine Garis Cochrane (1830–1913) invented the dishwasher in 1886. She was labeled a "socialite" on the grounds that she did not work outside her home and had servants to do her housework for her. Because these servants chipped the dishes they were washing, she produced the washing machine, which became the "hit" at the 1893 World's Columbian Exposition. Nevertheless, a number of manufacturers refused to produce her invention because she was a woman. She therefore gave her inventions to a temperance restaurant, leading to widespread acceptance of her invention. A wealthy woman, she organized the Cochrane Dishwasher Co., which later became KitchenAid and yet later became Whirlpool.[37]

Ruth Handler (1910–2002) invented the Barbie Doll and became co-founder of Mattel, the largest toy manufacturer in America. The name Mattel was produced by Ruth using part of the name of Harold Matson, also a co-founder of the toy company, and Elliot Handler, her husband. Barbie has become an American icon. The doll has been altered a number of times and has recently appeared in multi-cultural forms. The Mattel Co. grew immensely after the Handlers advertised on the Mickey Mouse show. It is now one of the Fortune 500 companies, earing $6.480 billion in 2013.[38]

Hedwig Kiesler, a.k.a. Hedy Lamarr, invented the Spread Spectrum, the technical basis for wireless communication in cell phones, faxes, integrated bar code scanners, modem devices, computer mail and other uses.

Originally, Kiesler-Lamarr's invention served as an anti-jamming device for use on radio-controlled torpedoes.

Kiesler was known as "the most beautiful woman in the world" during her long movie career as Hedy Lamarr. She had been married to an Austrian munitions manufacturer, whom she divorced at age 24. She then came to Hollywood where she appeared in thirty-four movies. She was married six times and had three children.[39]

Ellen Ochoa, Ph.D. is the Director of the Johnson Space Center in Houston, Texas. An astronaut, she invented an optical system designed to detect imperfections in repeating patterns. This invention can be used for quality control in the manufacture of numerous intricate machined parts. She also invented an optical system that can be used to robotically manufacture goods.[40]

VII

Janet Napolitano was appointed president of the University of California in 2013 at a salary of $570,000. Napolitano is a professional politician who previously was Secretary of Homeland Security, a position created after the attack on the World Trade Center in 2001. She was also governor of Arizona and held lesser political offices in earlier years. This appointment, and many others, demonstrates that the presidents of colleges and universities are politicians who may have some academic credentials but whose principal purpose is the raising of money from alumni and others. Napolitano has no academic experience whatever. She has never taught in any college, nor has she ever held an administrative position in any institution of higher education.[41]

Another female university president is Any Gutman, president of the University of Pennsylvania. She is paid more than $2 million. Gutman has an academic background and holds a doctorate in political science. She is married to a Columbia University professor of political science whose income is far from $2 million. Because the University of Pennsylvana is a private school, it is the most important task of the president to raise money from alumni.

Unlike CEO's in business and industry, university presidents have no impact on either students or faculty because the university is too diverse to make that possible. No president can know every subject matter from Anthropology to Zoology. This alone defeats any effort by a college president to supervise faculty, who have expertise in these many fields. Moreover, college and university faculty are in fact the management of the institution, as decided by the Supreme Court in the case of the so-called "Yeshiva Decision," which held that professors are in fact management and that therefore administrators need not bargain collectively with any union.

Another example of the political nature of college presidencies was the appointment of Kerry M. Healey as president of Babson College, located in Wellesley, Massachusetts. Healey was previously Lt. Governor of Massachusetts and earlier held numerous other political appointments in that state. She does have academic credentials, having earned a doctorate in political science in Ireland.

Likewise, Kimberly Cline has been named president of Long Island University, Kathleen McCartney has become president of Smith College, Nancy Roseman is president of Dickinson College, Jackie Scott is president of Wheelock College, Maria Hernandez Ferrier is president of Texas A&M University, and Drew Faust is president of Harvard University.

Faust earns more than $1 million a year. Divorced from her first husband, Stephen Faust, she is married to Charles Rosenberg, a history professor at Harvard, with whom she has one daughter. His salary is at the most $250,000 annually, because that is the highest salary Harvard pays a professor.

Catherine Drew Gilpin Faust is best described as an academic politician. The daughter of privilege, she was educated at the Concord Academy, a school restricted to America's upper class. Her father, McGhee Tyson Gilpin, was a Virginia "aristocrat" and descendant of two pilgrims who arrived in New England on the "Mayflower" in 1620. She also has two ancestors related to the British royal family. She is also a direct descendant of the Rev. Jonathan Edwards, no doubt the most famous preacher of his day. She is also distantly related to Theodore Roosevelt, Franklin Roosevelt, both Presidents Bush, Hugh Hefner, Clint Eastwood, and Eli Whitney, as well as Secretary of State John Kerry.

Faust graduated from Bryn Mawr College, an exclusive school for upper class women, and later earned a doctor's degree at the University of Pennsylvania.[42]

Barbara Snyder is president of Case Western Reserve University, located in Cleveland, Ohio. She earns more than $1.1 million. Snyder is a lawyer who graduated The University of Chicago School of Law. Subsequently she became an associate of a Chicago law firm and then moved on to become Provost at Ohio State University, having previously served on the faculty of the law school of Case Western Reserve University. After her appointment as president of CWRU, she joined innumerable organizations as board member or contributor. Snyder is credited with "turning CWRU around after having incurred heavy losses during the tenure of the previous president."

Snyder is married to Michael J. Snyder, with whom she has three children.[43]

Currently (2015) women have a better chance of becoming college presidents than men. Indeed, only 23% of college presidents are women. Yet, this is an immense increase, if judged against the lack of women in college presidencies twenty years ago. No doubt, boards of trustees who appoint college presidents are eager to appoint a woman and can do so because women are gradually outpacing men in attaining a higher education and achieving graduate degrees.

The evidence is that college and university presidencies are restricted to women or minorities or both and that so called "white" men need not apply.

It is evident from the above that women are gradually moving into the top echelons of American industry, business and educational institutions. This is also true of government, religion and communication media. The reason for this immense change in the empowerment of American women is primarily education, which is without doubt the ladder to success in American life.

Summary

Although the ascendancy of American women is not complete, as female income still lags behind that of men, it is evident that women have made considerable progress in attaining leading positions in industry and commerce. This is mainly due to the advances women have achieved in education, which is a prerequisite for success in American business.

Some consequences of these changes are that marriage is not as attractive to women who earn large incomes as it was when women could hardly find lucrative work. The employment of single and married women also has an impact on their children.

Women have demonstrated competence as CEO's of large companies, as business owners, as physicians, and as lawyers, as well as members of erstwhile all male occupations such as engineer or pharmacist.

Notes

1.U.S. Bureau of Labor Statistics. 2013. Annual Social and Economic Supplements to the Current Population Survey.

2. Catherine Rampless. "U.S. Women on the Rise as Family Breadwinners." The New York Times, (March 29. 2013):Business Day:1.

3. Pew Research Center Analysis of the Decennial Census and American Community Surveys

4. Ibid.

5. James T. Bond. Ellen Galinsky and Jennifer E. Swanberg. "The National Study of the Changing Workforce. New York. (Families and Work Institute. 1998). n.p.

6. Alex Heckert and Thomas C.Nowak. "The Impact of Husbands and Wives Relative earnings on marital disruption." Journal of Marriage and the Family. vol. 60. (1998), pp.690–703.

7. John L. Potucheck. Who Supports the Family? (Stanford . CA: Stanford University Press, 1997).

8. Rosalind Barnett and J.B. James. "The psychological effects of work experiences and disagreements about gender role beliefs in dual earner couples." Women's Health: Research on Gender. Behavior and Policy. Vol.4. (1998):341–348.

9. Lisa Cohen. Joseph P. Broschak and Heather A. Haveman. "And then there were more? American Sociological Review. vol. 36. (1998):711–727.

10. U.S. Census Bureau. (2011) Percentage of Managers in the Private Sector Who Are Female. 1970–2010 . Table 604.

11. Justin Wolfers. "Diagnosing Discrimination," Journal of the European Economic Association. vol.4, no.3. (April-May 2006):531–541.

12. National Center for Educational Statistics. "Digest of Education Statistics." Table 604. (2011).

13. Ann M. Beutel and and Margaret M. Marini, "Gender and Values." American Sociological Review, vol.60, (1995):436–438.

14. U.S. Bureau of the Census. Statistical Abstract of the United States. 2011. Washington, DC: U.S. Government Printing Office. Table 600.

15. Marianne Bertrand, et.al. "Dynamics of the gender gap for young professionals in the financial and corporate sectors. American Economics Journal: Applied Economics. vol. 2. (2010):228–255.

16. Hannah-Hanh D. Nguyen and Marie Ryan. "Does stereotype threat affect test performance of minorities and women?" Journal of Applied Psychology. vol. 93. (2008):1314–1334.

17. Judith Treas and Eric D. Widmer. "Married women's employment over the life course," Social Forces vol.78, (2000):1409–1436.

18. Jeanne Brett and Linda K. Stroh. "Working 61 plus hours a week. Why do managers do it? Journal of Applied Psychology. vol.86, (2003):67–78.

19. Annette Lareau and Elliott Weininger. "Time. Work and Family Life." Sociological Forum. vol. 23, (2008) :419–454.

20. Mary Blair-Loy. Competing Devotions. (Cambridge, MA: Harvard University Press. 2003).

21. Paul G. Davies. Stephen J. Spencer and Claude M. Steele. "Clearing the air" Journal of Personality and Social Psychology. vol.88. (2005):276–287.

22. No author, "Ten Things You Didn't Know About Women Owned Businesses" http://mashable.com/2012/08/14/facts-women-business (accessed April 14. 2015).

23. Ibid.:3.

24. Bill Vlasic, "New G.M. Chief Is Company Woman, Born To It." The New York Times, (December 12, 2013):Business Day :1.

25. No author. "Irene Blecker Rosenfeld is the CEO of Kraft Foods. Inc.." The Telegraph. (June 10. 2014):1.

26. Michael Ledtke. "Hewlett-Packard CEO Meg Whitman Gets Raise from $1 to $1.5 Million.

27. Carol Hymowitz and Sarah Frier. "IBM's Rometty Breaks Ground as Company's First Female Leader," Bloomberg Business Week. (October 26. 2011):1

28. http://www.bloomberg.com/research/stocks/people/person.asp ?personId=7785847&ticker=1137:HK (accessed April 14. 2015)

29. No author, Journal of the American Medical Association. "Wage Gap Persists for Women Physicians-Researchers." (June 15. 2012).

30. Kelli Woodhouse. Ann Arbor News. (May 16. 2014):1.

31. Ben Gose. "Red Cross Appoints New CEO". The Chronicle of Philanthropy. (April 8. 2008):1.

32. "Nancy Brinker." Encyclopedia of World Biography 2007 Supplement (Farmington Hills, MI: Gale, 2007)

33. Matthew Jaffe, "Boys and Girls Club CEO Roxanne Spillett's $1M Total Compensation Under Fire," ABC News. (March 12. 2010).

34. No author, A Current Glance at Women in the Law. Chicago: The American Bar Association, (2013):2–5.

35. Ibid.:6.

36. Ibid.:7.

37. J.M. Fenster, "The Woman Who Invented the Dishwasher," Inventions and Technology, (February, 1999):54–61.

38. Jacqueline Shannon, "Dream Doll: The Ruth Handler Story," Stamford, CT: Longmeadow Press, (1995).

39. Richard Rhodes. Hedy's Folly: The Life and Breakthrough Inventions of Hedy Lamarr, (New York: Doubleday, 2012).

40. No author, "Ellen Ochoa," National Aeronautic and Space Administration. Houston, TX, (2013).

41. Seth Zweifler, "University of California gets an unexpected leader in Janet Napolitano," The Chronicle of Higher Education. (July 18, 2013):1.

42. No author, "Drew Faust" Boston Business Journal. (May 19, 2014).

43. Peggy Turbett, "Case Western Reserve university president, Barbara Ann Snyder, is well compensated." The Cleveland Plain Dealer. (December 16, 20+13):28.

Chapter Two

Education and Female Achievements

I

It is evident that education is the ladder to success in the American economy. It therefore follows that the advances made by American women in the economic sphere as well as in all other social institutions is largely related to the ever increasing achievements of women in gaining more and more education. The evidence is that men are continuing to graduate from high school and college at a rate similar to that of earlier generations and that women are exceeding the attainment of men in every area of educational success.

Although 85% of high school age Americans attend high school, the number of boys who drop out of high school without graduating is higher than among girls. Girls drop out of high school at a ratio of one in four. Boys drop out at a ratio of one in three.[1]

This excess of male over female dropouts influences the rate of college admissions, because more women than men are eligible to enter higher education.

This skewed gender relationship has existed for over thirty-five years, beginning in 1979, when women first outnumbered men in higher education. Federal data show that 57% or more of students enrolled in institutions of higher education are female. This holds true in two year colleges as well as four year institutions and on the graduate level.

Ivy League universities, whose tuition is more expensive than that of other colleges, also exhibit this trend. At Brown University, 53% of students are female; at Cornell it is 59%, and at the University of Pennsylvania 51.1% of students are women. At Yale, the ratio of women to men is 52% to 48%. Princeton has a policy of admitting fifty percent of each gender and it is only at Columbia (52% to 48%) and Dartmouth (51% to 49%) that men outnumber women.[2]

The overall gender imbalance in American colleges has been 58% in favor of women to 42% for men among the 16.6 million college students currently enrolled. It is estimated that by 2017 the ratio of women to men will become sixty to forty.[3]

Moreover, the Bureau of Labor Statistics reports that by age 24, twenty-eight percent of women and 19% of men have earned a bachelor's degree. At age 27, thirty-two percent of American women have earned a bachelor's degree. Only 24 percent of men have a degree at age twenty-seven.[4]

One consequence of this imbalance is the recent effort of some college admissions directors to apply "affirmative action" to men. This means that some colleges try to entice men by adding engineering programs to their curricula, although the tradition of having mainly men enroll in engineering is being challenged by a considerable number of women now seeking engineering degrees.

Of the 472,000 American engineers, about 18%, or 85 thousand, are women. This appears to be a small representation of women within the profession. However, it also represents a major step forward in the employment of women in this area, as the number of women in engineering before the middle of the 20th century was negligible and nearly unknown before that. The fact is that female participation in science, technology, engineering, and mathematics is greater in the second decade of the 21st century than ever before.

In 2009, about one quarter of all STEM professionals were women. Those women who are employed in these fields earn an average of 33% more than women earn in all other areas of employment.

In an effort to increase the number of women seeking to enter mathematics generated professions, the U.S. government allocated $4.35 million in 2009 to encourage states to promote more interest in mathematics oriented areas of employment, with special emphasis on the participation of women.[5]

The Girl Scouts of the USA and the National Aeronautics and Space Administration have developed a memorandum of understanding to the effect that NASA will participate in the annual convention of GSUSA and allow "hands on" NASA STEM activities to encourage girls to become interested in science, technology, engineering and mathematics.

The Department of Education has a fund called "Invest in Innovation" which delivers grants to girl students who have demonstrated achievements in STEM subjects. These grants are used to further the interest of girls in mathematics related careers by enrolling in advanced education related to STEM. This initiative was augmented by a 2013 STEM "Education Strategic Plan" designated to bolster the participation of girls and women in studying STEM subjects.

One outcome of all these efforts is that in 2013 women earned 41% of Ph.D.'s in STEM fields, although they make up only 28% of tenure track faculty.

Female undergraduates in STEM subjects are offered monthly meetings with female mentors who are established in engineering and other sciences.[6]

II

The Association for Women in Mathematics seeks to encourage women to enter an area of education at one time nearly closed to women in this country. Although a good deal of effort has been made to recruit more women into mathematics, women are only twenty-seven percent of all mathematics majors in the U.S. This appears as a minuscule number. However, it is three times greater than was true in 1960, so that this percentage reflects some success in recruiting women into mathematics.[7]

Yet, today (2015) women are distinguishing themselves in this oldest and most important area of scientific inquiry. Indeed, there have been women mathematicians even among the most ancient times. Nevertheless it has only been during the second half of the 20th century that girls have been told in school that mathematics are not only for boys, a message teachers related almost universally in American schools for years.

As a result, more and more women study mathematics, alone because engineering and other scientific endeavors depend on knowledge of mathematics.This is attained by first earning a B.Sc. in mathematics. The University of Indiana mathematics curriculum is an example of the requirements to achieve this degree. Included in the courses available to graduate are: "Calculus," "Linear Algebra," "Discrete Mathematics," "Mathematical Reasoning," "Modern Algebra," "Introduction to Analysis," "Euclidian Geometry," "Probability," "Differential Equations," "Statistics," "Number Theory," "Metric Space Topology," and some computer courses.

As more and more women engaged in mathematics, the number of outstanding female mathematicians has increased. Karen E. Smith is one example of an exemplary achiever in mathematics. Smith graduated from Princeton University in 1987 with a degree in mathematics. After teaching a few years, she earned a Ph.D. in mathematics from the University of Michigan in 1993. Subsequently she became an instructor at the Massachusetts Institute of Technology. In 1997, she and her husband and three children moved to Michigan, where she teaches algebraic geometry at the University of Michigan. In 2001, Karen Smith was awarded the Ruth Lytle Satter prize in recognition of her work in commutative algebra. She has written a book on algebraic geometry.[8]

Freda Porter, a native American and member of the Lumbee tribe of North Carolina, earned a Ph.D. in mathematics from Duke University in 1991. Subsequently she taught at Pembroke State University. There she founded the American Indian Science and Engineering Society, which seeks to support native Americans and Alaskans to enter the STEM (science, technology, engineering, mathematics) areas of study. She is also president and CEO of "Porter Scientific, Inc." which deals with environmental issues.[9]

Nancy Margaret Reid earned a Ph.D. from Stanford University with a concentration on statistics. She has been University Professor of Statistics at the University of Toronto for several years. She has been instrumental in promoting the foundations of statistical inference and has made many other important contributions to statistics. She has held a number of offices in several mathematical societies and has published a great deal. As a result she was awarded the Parzen Prize by Texas A&M University and the David Award as well as the gold medal of the Statistical Society of Canada. She has a husband and two children.[10]

Linda Preiss Rothschild earned a B.A. in mathematics from the University of Pennsylvania in 1966 and a Ph.D. in Mathematics from M.I.T. in 1970. She then taught at Tufts University and later at Columbia University, Princeton University and the Institute for Advanced Studies. After a short stay at the University of Wisconsin, she became professor of mathematics at the University of California, San Diego. She worked on writing algorithms for factoring polynomials over the integers. Later she has been interested in the geometric aspects of several complex variables.

Rothschild has been President of the Association of Women in Mathematics and Vice President of the American Mathematical Society. In addition she has been the editor of a number of mathematics journals and served on the boards of a number of professional organizations. She is active in encouraging young women to enter the field of mathematics.

Rothschild is the widow of the mathematics professor Salah Baouendi, with whom she had two sons.

Physics is an area of study and investigation which had hardly any female representation before the twentieth century. Physics was hardly woman friendly as late as the first half of that century because of the beliefs concerning girls and women involved in mathematics based sciences. Here we are reminded of William I. Thomas who wrote in 1928: "If men define situations as real they are real in their consequences." [11]

The increase in female participation in physics may be seen by inspecting a chart depicting the growth of female physics students in high school. According to the American Institute of Physics, there were 243,000 female physics students at all U.S. high schools in 1987. This number rose to 379,000 in 1997, and reached 636,000 in 2009. 1,300 women attained a bachelor's degree in physics in 2011. [12]

An example of the courses taught to physics undergraduate students is the curriculum of the physics department at American University in Washington, D.C. These courses include: "Physics for the Modern World," "College Physics," "Principles of Physics," " Physics for a New Millennium," "General Physics," "Astronomy," "Changing View of the Universe," "Acoustics", "Electronics," "Waves and Optics," "Astrophysics," "Mathematical Physics," "Classical Mechanics," "Electricity and Magnetism," "Statistical Mechanics," "Quantum Mechanics," "Independent Study," "Capstone Seminar." [13]

As the number of female high school students interested in physics increased, the number of college students so inclined increased as well, reaching nineteen percent of physics students in 2013.

The American Physical Society includes a Committee on the Status of Women in Physics, which promotes the recruitment and career development of women in physics. The organization also features a woman physicist of the month. [14]

The entrance of women into physics has already led to the promotion of women into the upper levels of American industry, education and research. The list of prominent women in physics is considerable and includes Noemie Beczer Koller, a pioneer in nuclear and condensed matter physics, Louise Dolan, who contributed to particle physics by using Kac-Moody algebra, and Maria Goppert Mayer (1900–1972) who won the 1963 Nobel prize in physics. [15]

The study of chemistry has a long history in the United States. In 1876, thirty-five chemists founded the American Chemical Society in New York City. In 2013, that number had increased to 121,000. Thirty-nine percent of chemists are women. That contrasts remarkably with the eight percent of female chemists in 1960.[16]

Evidently, more women than ever before have decided to earn degrees in chemistry. An example of the course requirements to attain that degree is the curriculum at the University of Virginia. Included in these courses are: "Introduction to College Chemistry," "Principles of Chemical Structures," Organic Chemistry," "Calculus," "Ordinary Differential Equations," "Laboratories," "Thermodynamics and Quantum Theory," "Inorganic Chemistry," "Biological Chemistry," "Analytical Chemistry," and a number of other courses.[17]

Among women chemists are some outstanding contributors to American chemistry such as Carolyn Bertozzi (1960–) who designs artificial bones which do not cause rejection. She also created contact lenses which are better tolerated by the eye.

Bertozzi received the MacArthur "genius award" at age thirty-three. Her father, William Bertozzi, is a physicist, and her sister is a University of California mathematician. Carolyn Bertozzi is professor of chemistry at both the University of California at Berkeley and at the University of California at San Francisco.

Bertozzi studies glycobiology, which deals with diseases such as cancer, arthritis, and infectious diseases such as tuberculosis. She has received numerous awards and major recognition from her peers.

Laura Kiessling earned a Ph.D. in chemistry at Yale University and is a professor at the University of Wisconsin. She studies proteins in the human body and designs molecules that mimic various natural molecules that are part of the life of the body's cells.

Mildred Cohn (1910–2009) was a child prodigy, graduating from high school at age fourteen. She earned a Ph.D. in chemistry from Columbia University. She applied for an assistantship but was refused because she was a woman. She then studied under Harold Ury, who had won the Nobel Prize. Married to Henry Primakoff, she was appointed a researcher at George Washington University in St. Louis, where her husband had accepted an appointment. She became a pioneer in nuclear magnetic resonance.

After distinguishing herself in chemistry, she was appointed an associate professor of biochemistry at the University of Pennsylvania and was promoted to professor in 1961. She was elected to the National Academy of Sciences in 1971.

In the course of her career, Cohn wrote 160 papers, for which she was awarded a number of medals and other recognitions, including the National Medal of Science presented by President Ronald Reagan. Cohn and Primakoff had three children.[18]

Among all the STEM (Science, Technology, Engineering and Mathematics) areas of research, biology is most popular with women. About one half of all biology graduate students are women, and forty percent of biology postdoctoral fellowships are awarded to women. Nevertheless, only 36% of assistant professors of biology are women, and only 18% of professors are women.[19]

In 2013, women earned the majority of bachelor's and masters degrees and one half the doctor's degrees in biology. Between 1997 and 2007, there was a 16% increase in the number of women who graduated in biology, even as the number of men who graduated in biology decreased.[20]

Case Western Reserve University offers a biology degree, including these core courses: "Genes, Evolution and Ecology," "Cells and Proteins," "Development and Physiology," "Molecular Biology," "Fundamental Immunology," "Stem Cell Biology," "Plant Genomics," "Structural Biology," "Parasitology," "Microbiology," "Genes, Embryos, and Fossils," "Neurobiology," "Drugs, Brain and Behavior," "Aquatic Biology," and a number of other courses.[21]

About 86,000 students graduate in biology each year. Fifty-eight percent of these graduates are women, who earn a beginning salary of $40,000 to $50,000 annually. Those who earn a Ph.D. degree in biology seek research appointments, which are most precarious, as biology researchers depend on grants from foundations or government agencies for their income. Moreover, the pharmaceutical industry has laid off 300,000 biologists and outsourced these jobs to India and China. When these sources "dry up," the researchers lose their jobs and may be forced out of the profession in mid-career, as they are not re-employed when money is again available. Then new graduates are appointed and those laid off earlier are rejected.[22]

One of the most important female achievers in biology was Barbara McClintock (1900–1992). In 1983 she won the Nobel Prize in Physiology or Medicine for her discovery of mobile genetic elements or "jumping genes." She was also awarded the National Medal of Science, the Albet Lasker Award for Basic Medical Research; the Wolf Prize in Medicine, the Louise Gross Horwitz Prize from Columbia University, and the Thomas Hunt Morgan Medal by the Genetics Society of America.

McClintock earned three degrees from Cornell University, including a Ph.D. in biology. She spent the majority of her professional life at the Carnegie Institution in Washington, DC.[23]

Linda B. Buck and her professor, Richard Axel, were awarded the Nobel Prize in Physiology or Medicine in 2004. Buck and Axel showed how odors are perceived and identified. Buck earned a Ph.D. in immunology from the University of Texas in 1980, and in 2001 became professor of neurobiology at Harvard University.[24]

Elizabeth Blackburn was awarded the Nobel Prize in Physiology or Medicine in 2009. She shared this prize with Carol Greider and Jack Szostak for the discovery of how chromosomes are protected by telomeres and the enzyme telomerase. Blackburn, a native of Australia, moved to the United States after earning a Ph.D. in England. In California, she joined the faculty of the University of San Francisco after serving several years at the University of California at Berkeley.

Blackburn and Greider were credited by overenthusiastic journalists for finding a cure for cancer and reversing the aging process. None of this has developed, as journalists are ignorant and seek sensations.

Blackburn and Greider have been awarded the Lasker Medical Reserch Award and have been cited by TIME magazine among the "100 Most Influential People." Blackburn is married to Professor John Sedat, who teaches biochemistry at the University of San Francisco. They have one son.

Rosalind Franklin was responsible for the discovery of the double helix structure of DNA. There can be little doubt that she would have been awarded the Nobel Prize had she lived long enough and had she not been defrauded by two colleagues, Watson and Crick, who claimed to have made this discovery. Franklin died of ovarian cancer at age thirty-seven. Her contributions were denied by those who benefited by pretending her work was the work of others. As a result, numerous encyclopedias and other sources of scientific information have ignored Franklin's work and attributed her findings to Watson and Crick. In recent years, several authors have attempted to correct this injustice by writing books and producing television programs about Franklin's life. She was born in London, England and remained single. She earned a doctorate in chemistry from Cambridge University in 1945.[25]

A number of other women in biology have distinguished themselves over the years. Included are Martha Chase, Nicole Karafyllis, Nettie Stevens, and Ruth Turner. Because women have had a considerable interest in biology, it is not surprising that this has translated into a major movement of women into medicine and dentistry.

III

There are about 838,000 active physicians in the United States, according to the Statistical Abstracts of the U.S. (2012). Approximately 30% of these doctors are women. This is true of the entire physician cohort as of 2012. It is however evident that the percentage of women in medicine will rise considerably in the near future because the number of women now enrolled in medical schools as well as those recently graduated is a good deal greater.

Thus, in 2012, 47.3% or 20,780 of all applicants to medical schools were women. Of all female applicants, 9,787 or 47.1% were accepted. In that same year, 8,285 or 47.8% of all medical school graduates in the United States were women. In 1965 only nine percent of medical graduates were women.[26]

The curriculum for first year medical students includes gross anatomy, cell biology, metabolism and nutrition, molecular and population genetics, biostatistics and epidemiology, host defenses and hematology.

Students are later introduced to body systems. These are cardiovascular, gastrointestinal, renal, musculoskeletal, pulmonary, neuropsychological, endocrine and reproductive.

Courses which teach physicians to communicate with patients include medical interviewing, physical and mental status evaluation, human behavior in illness, medical ethics, caring for patients with social needs, risk factor assessment and intervention and care of patients across the lifespan.

In the third year of medical school, students are trained in hospitals where six "clerkships" are taught. These are medicine, surgery, obstetrics-gynecology, family medicine, pediatrics and psychiatry.

The fourth year includes study in such specialties as anesthesiology, radiation oncology, neurosurgery, and numerous others.[27]

The growth of female applicants to medical schools compared to that of men is attributed by some researchers to be the product of boys' relative educational under-performance, although the pre-admission scores of male applicants to medical schools do not support this view. Another possible reason for a decline in male interest in gaining a medical education may lie in the lucrative opportunities available in the business world as well as information technology and other areas.[28]

Yet, the most important reason for the increase in female applications to medial schools is the attainment of considerable scholarly competence by female applicants. An example is Sophia Balderman, M.D. who graduated suma cum laude from the University of Buffalo in 2004 with a degree in the biological sciences. Consequently she was cited for her outstanding performance in organic chemistry, and in addition earned fifteen awards in her medical career at State University College of Medicine at Syracuse, N.Y. After completing an internship in internal medicine at Strong Memorial Hospital in Rochester, N.Y. Sophia Balderman accepted a hematology fellowship leading to an appointment in hematology/oncology at Roswell Park Memorial Institute in Buffalo, N.Y.

Despite this considerable increase in female participation in medicine, many women doctors continue to complain of gender discrimination in the profession. These complaints are most common in academic medicine, in which doctors are employees and are not independent. Complainants claim that women are more often than men assigned work during major holidays and are expected to cover for the absence of others. Some women have said that they are assigned committee work, which takes time away from the research required for career advancement. Women are reputedly given fewer raises than men. Some women medical professors have reported incidents of sexual harassment, while others claim they are paid less than their male colleagues and are seldom promoted. A recent study has shown that women medical faculty members feel marginalized and ignored.[29]

There are some American women physicians who have made their mark on the profession. Among these is Ellen S. Baker, who earned an M.D. from Cornell University in 1978. In 1981 she joined NASA (National Aeronautics and Space Administration). There she served as a physician at the Johnson Space Center. In 1985, after considerable training, she became an astronaut. Since then, she has logged over 686 hours in space. She 1989 she flew 79 orbits around the earth in 119 hours. She also participated in the Columbia flight in 1992, and the Atlantis flight in 1995.[30]

Nancy Andrews, M.D., Ph.D. is dean of the Duke University School of Medicine and Vice Chancellor for Academic Affairs. She is also Nanaline H. Duke Professor of Pediatrics and Professor of Pharmacology and Cancer Biology. Before coming to Duke, Dr. Andrews was Professor of Pediatrics at Harvard Medical School, Senior Associate in Medicine at Children's Hospital Boston, and Distinguished Physician of the Dana-Farber Cancer Institute. Dr. Andrews was also director of the Harvard-MIT Ph.D. program and dean of the Basic Sciences and Graduate Studies at Harvard Medical School.

For thirteen years, Dr. Andrews was an investigator of the Howard Hughes Medical Institute. She has received numerous prizes and awards for research and served as president of the American Society of Clinical Investigators. She is a Fellow of the American Association for the Advancement of Science.

Dr. Andrews earned a B.S. and M.S. degrees in Molecular Biophysics and Biochemistry from Yale University and a Ph.D. in Biology from MIT and an MD from the Harvard Medical School.

Dr. Andrews is married to Dr. Bernard Mathey-Prevot, with whom she has two children, Camille and Nicholas.

In 1998, Dr. Nancy Dickey was the first woman to have been elected president of the American Medical Association. In that role she traveled 170 days a year on AMA business. Born Nancy Wilson in South Dakota in 1950, she moved to Texas and graduated with a degree in psychology. After marrying Frank Dickey, she enrolled in the University of Texas Medical School, graduating in 1976. She had three children before finishing her residency. In 1996, she was appointed associate director of family medicine at Texas A&M University. After ending her term as president of the AMA, she was appointed president of A&M University System Health Sciences. She now holds a number of offices within the health system. She has received a number of honors, including a medal from the Texas Society of Pathologists and a listing in America's Best Doctors.

Beatrice H. Hahn M.D. is professor of medicine at the University of Pennsylvania Perelman School of Medicine. In 2012, she was elected to the National Academy of Sciences for her work on human pathogens. She has been honored by the Institute of Medicine of the National Academies and was cited as one of the 50 most important women in science.

Hahn was born in Munich (München), Germany, where her father was a physician who allowed her to assist him. She graduated from the University of Munich with a degree in medicine (M.D.). She is married to George Shaw, who is also a professor of medicine.

Since women are gradually becoming the majority of physicians, the chances that a woman will treat a patient are becoming more and more certain. This is also true of pharmacists, as women now constitute 67% of that profession. Since 91.1% of nurses are women, it can be predicted with confidence that the entire American health delivery system is already or will shortly be feminized.

There has also been a considerable increase in the number of women in dentistry since the 1990's. Since then, the number of female dentists has increased by at least 35% and is growing. This is visible by considering the increase in the number of female dental students. Overall, one half of dental students in 2014 were women. In fifteen schools of dentistry, women outnumber men. There are 57 schools of dentistry in the United States. About 12 thousand students applied to dental schools in the United States in 2010, up from about 7,700 in 2000, an increase of 55%.[31]

An example of the curricula in American schools of dentistry is the list of courses taught at the University of Louisville School of Dentistry. The first year student enrolls in "Gross and Neuroanatomy," "Histology," "Physiology," "Dental Anatomy and Occlusion," "Oral Radiology," "Head and Nose Anatomy," "Biochemistry," "Clinical Dentistry," "Growth, Development and Aging," Periodontics," Preventive Dentistry," "Cariology," "Cast Restoration," "General Pathology," and others.[32]

The acute shortage of primary care physicians in the United States has led to the creation of a new profession, I.e. Physician's Assistant. At present, 55% of physician's assistants are women. Since 72% of PA students are female, it is evident that this profession will shortly be overwhelmingly feminized. The median income of PA's is $84,000.[33]

As of 2013, there were 173 accredited physician's assistants programs in the United States. Another 65 programs were awaiting accreditation. These programs average 27 months year-round. They require one year of classroom and laboratory instruction and a second year of clinical experience. Approximately 44 students graduate from each program every year, so that in 2012 the graduating cohort was 7,200, a number projected to 9,000 within ten years (2023).[34]

Another fast growing profession is nurse practitioner. Of the 3.1 million registered nurses in the United States, 140,000 of these R.N.'s are nurse practitioners. Each year 6,474 people graduate as nurse practitioners, of whom no more than 6% are men. Registered nurses earn a median income of $61,300 per year. The median salary of nurse practitioners is $96,018, with some earning

$112,000. Universities which provide degrees for nurse practitioners include Walden University, The University of Phoenix, De Vry University, Baker College, Saint Joseph's University, and others, all of whom teach courses online.[35]

The curriculum at the University of Cincinnati leading to the master's degree needed to become a nurse practitioner includes "Biostatistics," "Theoretical Basis for Clinical Reasoning," "Health Care Policy", "Advanced Health Assessment," "Pharmacology," "The Care of Well Women and Children," Family Nurse Practitioner I," "Research and Best Evidence for Clinical Reasoning," "Differential Diagnosis," "Clinical Management," and "Seminar and Capstone."[36]

IV

In the early years of American history, women were not allowed to receive a higher education because it was believed that more than a rudimentary education for women was "unnatural" and that women who sought to achieve more education than "readin', writin' and 'rithmitic" were "unisexed."[37]

Because women were refused higher education for so many years, some wealthy Americans established all female colleges in the nineteenth century. One of these all female colleges is Bryn Mawr College, located in Bryn Mawr, Pennsylvania. The Welsh phrase "Bryn Mawr" means "big hill." The college was founded in 1885, largely financed by Joseph Taylor, a physician. The original purpose was to teach young women the principles of the Quaker faith. This was soon abandoned in favor of allowing the college to become non-denominational. Unlike the numerous "finishing schools" for girls, Bryn Mawr adopted a rigorous curriculum designed to equal that taught in any American university that admitted only men.

The college enrolled 1,200 undergraduates and 400 graduate students as of 2014. The cost of attending in 2014 was $58,165 per academic year, of which tuition alone amounted to $42,810. The other money covered room and board, various fees and dues. Evidently, this college is limited to the very wealthy, as few Americans can afford to pay over $232,000 for a four year education.[38]

Smith College, located in Northampton, MA, was founded in 1875 by means of a bequest of Sophia Smith, who had inherited a fortune. The first class consisted of 14 students and six faculty. The college enrolled 2,600 undergraduates and 102 graduate students in 2014. It has 285 faculty members and an endowment of $1.557 billion. Tuition, room and board, and fees amount to $59,614 per year, or $238,536 to attain a bachelor's degree.[39]

A third example of an all female college is Stephens College in Columbia, MO. It was founded in 1833 by Richard Gentry on the grounds of the Columbia Female Academy, which had 25 students and taught only English, moral philosophy, algebra, and geography. Later renamed the Columbia Female Baptist Academy, the school benefitted from an endowment of $20,000. This led the trustees to rename the college for its benefactor. Today the college enrolls 882 students. Two hundred and nine were graduate students in 2003. Tuition and all fees amount to $40,338. Today Stephens College has an aviation program for women and more recently introduced an online program leading to the M.B.A. degree and the M.Ed. degree.

There are numerous other women's colleges in the United States. These include Sweet Briar College, Mills College, Mount Holyoke College, Scripps College, Simmons College, Agnes Scott College, Barnard College, and many others.

Although wealthy women could escape the prejudices which prevented most women from gaining a higher education, beliefs concerning women's intellectual inferiority continued until the 1930's, when considerable changes in women's education at the college level began. Thus, in 1900, there were 85,338 female college students, of whom only 5,237 even earned a bachelor's degree. By 1940, there were 600,953 female college students in the United States, of whom 77,000 earned a bachelor's degree.[40]

In 2013 there were 12.5 million women enrolled in American undergraduate colleges compared to 9.3 million men.[41] According to Forbes Magazine, more women chose business as their major than any other of the top ten college majors chosen. Business was the major of 161,145 women in a 2010 survey, followed by health professions with 87,455 majors, education with 83,139, social sciences with 81,763, psychology with 69,690, arts, which was the major of 52,475 women, communications, the majors of which numbered 49,405, and biological sciences, numbering 45,166, followed by 32,648 English majors and 30,168 liberal arts and humanities majors.[42]

Business was also the first choice for men, although men chose engineering as a third option, a major which did not make the first ten majors among women.

A small number of women enrolled in the military academies of the United States armed forces in 1976. This came about after President Ford signed Public Law 106 which had been passed by congress and required the service academies to enroll women. At that time, 119 women entered The United States Military Academy at West Point, and 81 women entered the U.S. Naval Academy at Annapolis. More recently, all three academies enroll approximately 4000 to 4100 students, Of these, about 14% are women at West Point and Annapolis, and about 20% of the students at the Air Force Academy are women.

Traditionally, and even at the beginning of the 21st century, the majority of the 3,300,000 public school teachers have been women. As late as 2008, seventy-six percent of all American teachers were female. Seventy-four percent of female teachers had a master's degree and an equal number were under age forty. These teachers earned an average of $56,643 annually.

Those women who graduated from college in 2010–2012 were evidently more interested in business administration than in becoming teachers. While slightly more than 84,000 women attained degrees in education that year, over

190 thousand women earned degrees in business in 2010–2012. The health related professions attracted 139 thousand female majors, and psychology equaled the number enrolled in education. Even engineering, at one time closed to women, attracted over 17 thousand female majors. [43]

Nevertheless, elementary and secondary school teaching is still principally in the hands of women. In 2011, 81.1% of the 1,520,000 American elementary and middle school teachers were women, earning a median annual pay of $53,000.

The curriculum concerning a degree in teaching in an elementary school is well exhibited by the course requirements at The State University College at Buffalo, NY. That curriculum includes "Introduction to Elementary Education," "Child Development," "Educational Psychology," "Introduction to Literacy," Programs for Infants and Toddlers," "The Teaching of Reading," "Emergent Literacy," "Practicum in Teaching," "Parents, School and Community," Classroom Management," and others. [44]

There can be little doubt that the elementary school teacher is the most important teacher in that long chain of teachers employed from kindergarten through graduate school. If income were based on the effect elementary teachers have on nearly all Americans, then elementary teachers would earn a good deal more than anyone else participating in American education.

While the vast majority of elementary school teachers are women, women were 58.1% among the 955,000 secondary school teachers in 2011, earning $55,000 annually. [45]

About 46% of the 1,496,810 American college professors are women. Their median pay is $68,970. In recent years (2010–2014), less than 25% of college faculty have been tenured or are on a tenure track. There has been an 18% decline in financial support for higher education from the states, leading to the employment of part time, or so-called adjunct faculty, earning about $18,000 a year. These are mainly women. Moreover, full time women professors earned only 77.7% of male salaries. [46]

It is reasonable to project that the near future will reveal a far greater participation of women on the faculties of American universities. This is inevitable because for the first time in 2013 more women earned Ph.D.'s than is true of men. Including other academic doctorates such as the Ed.d., D.Sc. etc., 28,962 women and 28,469 men were granted such a degree in 2013. Women therefore achieved 50.4% of these degrees, up from 44% in 2000. It needs to be remembered that despite these achievements, women are still underrepresented in the high paying fields of engineering (21.6%), mathematics, and computer science, as well as in physical (26.8%) and earth sciences (33.4%). [47]

V

In 1972, nine percent of law students were women, but in 2010, fifty percent of law students were women. By 2010, women were admitted to all law schools in the United States. A typical curriculum at law schools included such areas of study as Law and Government; Law and Business; International Law; Law, Science and Technology; Law and Social Change; Criminal Justice, and Law and History.

At the Harvard University School of Law, the 2010–2015 list of courses included "Civil Rights Legislation", "International Law", "Rhetoric and Public Discourse," "Environmental Litigation," "Internet and Society," "Animal Law," "National Security Law," "Life after Conviction and Incarceration," "Great Negotiators," "Taxation," "Law and Medicine," "The Supreme Court," "The Modern Judiciary," "Interpreting the Constitution," "Corruption," "Housing Law," and many others including Islamic and other foreign law.[48]

In 2010, twenty percent of deans and 66% of assistant deans of law schools were women. In 2012, women constituted 31% of all lawyers. In 1995, only 13% of law partners were women. That figure rose somewhat, to 25% by 2011, and rose again to about 33% by 2014. About 8% of American lawyers work for federal, state or local governments; the others work in the private sector, and, of these, 48% are self-employed with no partner.

Although one half of all law students are women, it is evident that women have not achieved equality with men in the profession. Even among state and federal judgeships, only 23% of federal and 27% of state judges were women in 2011. Law firms are equally slow in appointing women to leading positions. In 2011, only 10% of firm chairpersons were women, and only 12% had female managing partners. The majority of lawyers in the United States are in private practice. This is true of 52% of women and 55% of men.[49]

The American Bar Association has been far more attentive to women than the profession in general. While women lawyers earned only 80% of men's incomes in 2012, four women have been elected president of the American Bar Association. The first was Roberta C. Ramo, the second Martha Barnett, the third Karen Mathis, and the fourth Carolyn Lamm.[50]

According to the Bureau of Labor Statistics, in 2014, thirty-three percent of the 1.092 million American lawyers were women. Because 46,405 law degrees were awarded in 2013 when there were only 24,640 job openings, it is evident that there are more lawyers in the country than can be accommodated.[51]

The National Association for Law Placement has shown that only 88% of law graduates in 2010 were employed one year after graduation. Among law graduates in 2012, only 84.5% had secured jobs after one year since graduation, with a median salary of $62,000, the lowest rate since 1996. Even lower salaries are reported, as some law firms pay only $10,000 and yet have numerous applicants from those who have no work at all. Meanwhile, law schools keep graduating more and more lawyers because they seek tuition dollars, even as clients of lawyers seek cheaper legal services. Many private law practitioners have cut their fees because of the immense competition.[52]

Law schools like to pretend that their graduates are fully employed. To support such claims, the law schools include graduates who are working in all kinds of jobs that do not require a law degree. As a result, a number of law schools are being sued by their former students. These law schools have raised their tuition and fees to an average of $39,000 a year, so that graduates often owe $156,000 to banks and other lenders even as they are unemployed.[53]

There are four women lawyers who have escaped all that, as their political acumen led them to reach the pinnacle of the legal profession by becoming associate judges on the Supreme Court of the United States. The first woman to be appointed to the Supreme Court was Sandra Day O'Connor, who was nominated by President Ronald Reagan in 1981. She participated in the important Planned Parenthood V. Casey decision, which affirmed the earlier Roe V. Wade decision permitting abortion throughout the U.S.A. A Republican, she served on the court for 24 years. In her earlier career, Sandra Day worked for free at the California County San Mateo county attorney's office just to get some experience, because she was unable to find a job for months after graduating from the Stanford University School of Law. O'Connor moved to Arizona and entered politics. She was twice elected to the state senate and was then elected judge in the Maricopa County court.[54]

The second woman to become a justice of the Supreme Court was Ruth Bader Ginsburg. Nominated by President Bill Clinton, she took office on August 10, 1993. Ginsburg had been a volunteer lawyer for the American Civil Liberties Union and was a professor of law at Rutgers University and the Columbia Law School. She was appointed to the Court of Appeals by President Jimmy Carter, where she served from 1980 until 1993. She has two children, Jane and James, with her husband Martin Ginsburg.[55]

Sonia Sotomayor waswas nominated by President Obama to become the third female justice of the Supreme Court in 2009. A graduate of Princeton University, she earned a law degree from Yale University. Subsequently she became a prosecutor and a judge in New York City.

Divorced without children, Sotomayor has been active in Democrat politics and was appointed in an effort to secure the Hispanic vote for the incumbent president.[56]

The fourth woman to be appointed to the Supreme Court is Elena Kagan. A graduate of Princeton University, she earned a law degree from the Harvard Law School, where she became a law professor after holding a similar position at the University of Chicago School of Law. Active in Democrat politics, she was Associate Council to the President for four years during the Clinton administration. After holding yet another political appointment, she became dean of the Harvard Law School and thereafter associate justice of the Supreme Court.[57]

No doubt the entrance of four women into the Supreme Court indicates that one more obstacle to the advance of women toward an American matriarchy has been achieved. This is true despite the difficulties law graduates of both sexes have encountered.

VI

The American Society of News Editors conducts an annual census concerning employment in the journalism profession. This census shows that the percentage of women employed in newsrooms was about 37% in 2012, a number which has been unchanged for fifteen years.

Women were most often employed as copy layout editors. In that occupation they constitute 42.3% of all such editors. Only 25% of photographers, artists, and videographers are women. Women reporters and writers constituted about 38%. This contrasts sharply with the fact that in 2011, 62.5% of journalism students were women, and that nationwide in 2014 this figure rose to 65% of students in journalism.[58]

The principal schools of journalism in the United States are the College of Journalism at the University of Florida, the Grady College of Journalism at the University of Georgia, the Indiana University School of Journalism, The University of Kansas School of Journalism, the University of Maryland Phillip Merrill College of Journalism, the University of Missouri School of Journalism, the University of North Carolina School of Journalism, Northwestern University Medill School of Journalism, Ohio University E.W. Scripps School of Journalism, and the Newhouse School of Public Communication at Syracuse University.[59]

The curriculum at the University of Florida College of Journalism includes twelve "core" courses. Among these are "Introduction to Journalism," "Mass Media and You," "Visual Journalism," "Writing Mechanics," "Multimedia Writing,"" Reporting," "Editing," Ethics in Journalism," and others. Numerous electives are also offered.[60]

The median income of newspaper reporters is $43,000 annually, with a beginning salary of about $35,700 and a salary for experienced reporters of approximately $61,000. Editors earn a median income of $46,000. Senior editors may earn $77,000, although some exceptional editors at a few nationally distributed newspapers may earn more. Female editors are about 43% of all editors, thirty-eight percent of reporters are women, and 27% of video and other artistic talent are women.[61]

There are some women who have succeeded as executive editors in print journalism. Among these is Jill Abramson Griggs, who was appointed executive editor at the New York Times in September 2011 and dismissed in May 2014. A Harvard graduate, Griggs worked for the Wall Street Journal and later became the Times Washington bureau chief. Her career as executive editor was short.

She was fired by Arthur Sulzberger, the publisher of the Times, on grounds having to do with her personal relations with co-workers. This is not unusual. In fact, the overwhelming majority of people fired from their jobs are dismissed because of personality issues.[62]

Donna Byrd was hired by the Washington Post and named the publisher of The Root. She received the Lucille Harris-Bluford Spotlight Award. A graduate of a German high school, she earned a B.A. in American Government from the University of Virginia and an M.B.A. from Duke University. She further studied business at the University of Cape Town in South Africa. She previously worked as sales manager at Proctor and Gamble, brand manager for the Coca Cola Co., and vice-president for Ez.Gov. She later developed Black America, an African-American news and entertainment website. She later became managing partner at Kickoff Marketing.[63]

Chrystia Freeland graduated from Harvard University with a degree in Russian history and literature. She then became a Rhodes Scholar and earned a master's degree in Slavonic Studies from Oxford University. Early in her career she wrote for The Financial Times, later becoming an editor and bureau chief in Moscow. She then became deputy editor for The Globe and Mail, where she also wrote a weekly column. Then she worked for Reuters in similar positions and then moved to New York City, where she became managing editor of The Financial Times. Freedland also wrote two books. She speaks English, French, Ukrainian, Russian and Italian.

She is married to Graham Bowley, a New York Times reporter, with whom she has three children.

More prominent than editors are newspaper columnists. Among the forty most prominent columnists in 2014, there were twelve women.

Michelle Malkin earned a B.A. degree at Oberln College in an effort to become a concert pianist. She changed her major to English and began her career as a columnist at the Los Angeles Daily News. She later moved to Seattle, where she wrote for the Seattle Times, and in 1999 she became a nationally syndicated columnist. She is the author of four books.

Malkin is married to Jesse Malkin, with whom she has two children. Mr. Malkin is a house husband who takes care of their children.[64]

Gail Collins is a columnist and member of the editorial board at the New York Times. Prior to joining the New York Times, Collins was a columnist at New York Newsday and the New York Daily News. Earlier she worked as a reporter for United Press International and then founded the Connecticut State News Service. Collins graduated from Marquette University with a B.A. in journalism and also earned an M.A. in government from the University of Massachusets. She is married to Dan Collins, who works for CBS News.[65]

Ann Coulter is a truly famous columnist, as she is one of the very few journalists holding non-liberal views and defending these views in her columns and at guest appearances on television. Coulter earned a B.A. from Cornell Uni-

versity and a J.D. law degree from the University of Michigan. She is a columnist for Universal Press. Editor of the Michigan Law Review, Coulter is a frequent public speaker and reputedly earns $500,000 a year for doing so. So far,
Coulter has written ten books. Her column is featured on six conservative web
sites. Coulter appears regularly on numerous TV and radio talk shows as well as
TV documentaries. She is not married.[66]

Women are well represented among television announcers and talk show
hosts. Of the 561,000 persons employed in broadcasting in the U.S. , 40.9%
were women, according to the Bureau of Labor Statistics. Women were 46.9%
of the 81,000 news analysts in 2012.[67]

No doubt the most successful woman among news broadcasters on television has been Katie Couric, who in 2006 became the first woman to anchor the
CBS evening news alone. Other women have since done the same on other
channels. After graduating from the University of Virginia, Couric started her
career at NBC, eventually becoming the co-host of Today, and later on Dateline,
for which she was paid $7 million for each of four years. In 2002, Couric signed
a deal with NBC which paid her $65 million over four and one half years. Her
show Katie was cancelled in July 2014. Thereupon Couric accepted an appointment with Yahoo which paid her $6 million a year.

Couric is the widow of Jay Monahan, with whom she had two children.
She married John Moler in 2014.[68]

Diane Sawyer is one of the most successful women in broadcasting. She
earned a B.S. degree in English at Wellesley College in 1967 and began her career as a weather forecaster in Louisville, Kentucky. Subsequently she became
an assistant to the White House press secretary in Washington, DC, which led
her to draft some of President Nixon's public statements. This in turn permitted
her to become staff assistant to the president. After Nixon's resignation she
moved to California and helped Nixon write his memoirs, which were published
in 1978. That year she returned to Washington and joined CBS. She became co-
anchor with Charles Kuralt on the morning news show. Later she moved to ABC
and co-anchored Primetime Live with Sam Donaldson. She held a number of
other jobs since 2000 and as of 2014 was the sole anchor at ABC's "World
News." She left that position in August of 2014 and continues to broadcast "spe-
cials." Forbes magazine estimates her earnings at $4 million a year. Sawyer is
married to Mike Nichols. She has no children.[69]

A somewhat unusual television journalist is Pamela Silva Conde. Born in
Peru, she earned a B.A. degree from Florida International University and an
M.B.A. at St. Thomas University. She won the Emmy Award for excellence in
journalism six times. She is co-anchor of Univision Network's weekday newsmagazine "First Impact," which is seen in the United States and in 12 Latin
American countries. Silva Conde has hosted numerous programs for Univision,
where she is the leading Spanish language morning newscaster. She is also an

investigative reporter for a newsmagazine. In addition to her Emmy awards, she was recognized as alumna of the year by her alma mater. [70]

VII

Few donors to American charities are aware that charity administrators can earn salaries far above $1 million and that incomes of $300,000 to $400,000 are commonplace. The reason for this explosion in compensation for charity executives lies in the history of welfare in America.

Prior to the Franklin D. Roosevelt administration, charity was entirely in the hands of private, voluntary organizations, as well as local politicians seeking votes and organized crime inducing people to gamble, all of whom furnished the poor and needy with food, clothing, and rent. These voluntary groups were largely unable to meet the consequences of the Great Depression beginning in 1929 and lasting until the outbreak of the Second World War in September of 1939.

In the 1930's, President Franklin Roosevelt and Congress initiated public relief financed by taxpayers. This began with the Social Security Administration, which facilitated the establishment of unemployment compensation, and provided aid to the blind, aid to children, and old age pensions.

Even as public assistance began to edge out private charities, the profession of social work first established itself in American colleges and universities. In 1898, the New York School of Philanthropy offered a summer session in social work, which became a two year full time program in 1910. This development was followed in Philadelphia, Chicago, and other large cities, and finally resulted in the degree of Master of Social Work, granted by a number of universities after 1930. [71]

Social work has always been primarily staffed by women, who make up 81% of the 642,000 American social workers, earning between $34,000 and $40,000 annually.

As social work became a profession supported by government, I.e. the taxpayers, private social work organizations became professional bureaucracies as well. These privately funded charities depend on the contributions of wealthy individuals who are compensated by "serving" on the boards of trustees and holding offices in these charities such as president, vice president, treasurer, secretary, etc. Such honorific positions are bought by wealthy persons who seek social honor. This is bestowed on them by "executive directors," "executive vice presidents," and other administrators, who are in turn paid large salaries dependent on the goodwill of wealthy contributors. Consequently, professional social workers whose incomes average in the vicinity of $37,000 learn that the road to high incomes in their profession lies in becoming an administrator and sycophant to those who make large contributions. Political acumen is therefore the means by which entrance to high salaries is achieved. Those who understand this are well rewarded.

Among those who attain CEO positions in various charities are a number whose income well exceeds $1 million. This can be substantiated by consulting a website called Charity Navigator. According to that research foundation, there are some male charity executives who are paid upward of $3 million, although that is unusual.

There are fewer women executives among charity administrators than male executives, although women are by far the majority of social workers in this country.[72]

Nevertheless, some women executives of charities are paid more than the President of the United States, who is responsible for the whole country for $400,000 annually. Thus, perhaps the most astonishing salary is that of Deborah Borda, who receives $920,232 for her role as manager of the Los Angeles Philharmonic Orchestra. It is of course doubtful whether a symphonic orchestra is a charity, although these orchestras usually ask for contributions from the public.Then there is Cory Cloninger, who heads "Girl Scouts of America" for $809,493, as Gail McGovern, executive of the American Red Cross, is paid $560,864. Vicki Escara, CEO of "Feeding America" collects $357,303, and Jilly Stevens, CEO of "City Harvest" is paid $388,309.

Here are more salaries enjoyed by female charity administrators: Carolyn Miles of "Save the Children" is paid $403,857 and Kathleen Kane at "City of Hope" gets $770,209. Nancy Brickman of the "Nancy Koren Foundation" is paid $684,000.

Numerous other female administrators of charities in this country collect more than $200,000, or at least $150,000. It is important to consider that executives invariably appoint at least two assistants who are paid commensurate salaries reflecting the income of the boss. Surely someone whose paycheck amounts to more than $600,000 pays an assistant one half that or more. As the payroll declines from the top to the average social worker, less and less is paid those who finally meet clients, for whom little if anything can be done, as the payroll has exhausted the resources of the charity.

Summary

More girls and women remain in high school and college than is true of boys and men. In recent years more and more women have graduated in science, technology, engineering, and mathematics than ever before. Women have recently earned degrees in physics, chemistry, and biology, and have become nearly half the graduates from medical and dental schools. Physician's assistants and nurses are mostly women, so that the health related occupations will soon become entirely feminized.

Although women have earned most of the education degrees, business degrees are now preferred by more women students than education degrees. Nevertheless, most teachers in grade and secondary schools are women, and more and more women are becoming professors, as a majority of new Ph.D. degrees are now earned by women.

Women have also entered the legal profession, which is so overrun with new graduates each year that numerous new lawyers have to find other means of earning their livelihoods.

Social work has been the province of women since its inception. Poorly paid, women are gradually succeeding in gaining administrative positions in charities, which pay upward of $200,000 and allow some administrators to collect more than a million dollars a year.

Not all occupational achievements by women in the last thirty years involve higher education. There are women who have entered areas of work once totally male dominated. There are few women in these occupations. Nevertheless it is significant that the Bureau of Labor Statistics lists that 6.2% of truck drivers are female, that 5.5% of airline pilots are women, and that 5.3% of machinists are female. Women account for 1.1% of highway maintenance workers and 1.6% of carpenters. 3.6% of construction workers are women and 1.8% of electricians are female, as are 1.1% of plumbers.[73]

All these successes by women have had a profound effect on the American family, as more and more women earn more than their husbands and men become housebound, raising children.

Notes

1. Ranit Schmelzer, "High School Dropouts: a Problem for Girls and Boys," Answer Bag," (Washington, DC: National Women's Law Center, October 30, 2007):1.

2. No author, "2014 Ivy League Admission Statistics," The Ivy Coach, (2014):1.

3. Nick Anderson, "The Gender Factor in College Admissions, The Washington Post, (March 26, 2014):1.

4. United States Department of Labor. Bureau of Labor Statistics. "America's Young Adults at 27," (March 26, 2014.):1.

5. No author, Women in STEM: a Gender Gap to Innovation. U.S. Department of Commerce, Economics and Statistics Administration, (August 2011):1.

6. Ibid.:1.

7. David Beede, et.al. "Women in STEM," U.S. Department of Commerce, (2009).

8. Larry Riddle, "Karen E. Smith," The Notices of the American Mathematical Society, vol.48, no.4, (April 2001):411–412.

9. Robert Hawthorne, Jr., "Freda Porter Locklear," American Indian Biographies, Harey Markovitz, Editor. (Salem Press, 1999):274–275.

10. Larry Riddle, "Nancy Reid," Biographies of Women Mathematicians, (Decatur, GA, 2013). http://www.agnesscott.edu/lriddle/women/reid.htm [accessed July 9, 2015].

11. William I. Thomas, The Child in America: Behavioral Problems and Programs, (New York: Knopf, 1928): 571–572.

12. Susan White, et. al. "Female Students in High School Physics," (College Park, MD: American Institute of Physics, 2011):1.

13. College of Arts and Sciences, American University: "Physics Courses," http://www.american.edu/cas/physics/courses.cfm [accessed April 30, 2015].

14. American Physical Society, "Women in Physics", (2014):1.

15. No author, Contributions of 20th Century Women to Physics, Washington DC, The American Physical Society, http://cwp.library.ucla.edu [accessed April 30, 2015].

16. U.S. Department of Labor, Bureau of Labor Statistics, Employed Persons by Sex, Race and Ethnicity, (2013):table 11.

17. http://chem.virginia.edu/undergraduate-studies-/chemistry-maj [accessed April 30, 2015].

18. William Theodore de Bary, Jerry Kisslinger, and Tom Mathewson, eds. Living Legacies at Columbia, (New York: Columbia University Press, (2006):208.

19. Sarah McDowell, "Research reveals a gender gap in the nation's biology labs," PhysOrg, June 30, 2012:1.

20. Perla Trevizo, "Women overtake men in earning degrees at all levels," Time Free Press, (February 21, 2012):1.

21. http://biology.case.edu/undergraduate/bachelor-of-arts-biology [accessed April 30, 2015].

22. Christopher Drew, "Where the Women Are," The New York Times, (April 4, 2011): Education 1.

23. Nina Federoff, "Barbara McClintock," Biographical Memoirs, vol. 68 (Washington, DC: The National Academy Press, 1995):211–230.

24. Jaqui Safra, "Linda B. Buck," Encyclopedia Britannica, (Chicago, IL: Merriam-Webster, 2004).

25. Brenda Maddox, Rosalind Franklin: The Dark Lady of DNA, (New York: Harper Collins, Publishers, 2002).

26. No author, "Tomorrow's Doctors: Tomorrow's Cures," (Washington, DC: Association of American Medical Colleges, (2013):Table 1.

27. University of Buffalo School of Medicine and Biological Sciences, MD Degree Curriculum, http://medicine.buffalo.edu/education/md/curriculum.html [accessed April 30, 2015].

28. Ralph A. Cooper, "Impact of trends in primary, secondary and post-secondary education on applicants to medical school," Academic Medicine, vol.78, no.9, (2003):855–863.

29. Pauline W. Chen, "Sharing the Pain of Women in Medicine," The New York Times, (November 29, 2012):D7.

30. Laura Woodmansee, Women Astronauts. Burlington, Ont., Apogee Books, (2002):70–71.

31. ADEA Survey of American Dental School Applicants. American Dental School Association, (2010).

32. http://louisville.edu/dentistry/degrees/dmd/curriculum/first-year [accessed April 30, 2015].

33. American Academy of Physician Assistants, National Physician's Assistants Study: Census Report, (Washington DC, 2013).

34. James T. Cawley et.al. "Physician Assistants in American Medicine," The American Journal of Managed Care, vol.19, no.10, (2013):1.

35. U.S. Department of Labor, Women's Bureau, Bureau of Labor Statistics.

36. University of Cincinnati, Family Nurse Practioner Curriculum," http://nursingonline.uc.edu/online-nursing-degree/nursing-specialties/family-nurse-practitioner/, accessed April 30, 2015.

37. John Rury, "Vocationalism for Home and Work: Women's Education in the United States, 1880–1930," History of Education Quarterly, vol. 24, no.1, (1984):39.

38. Allen Grove, "Bryn Mawr College," Top Women's Colleges in the United States, http://collegeapps.about.com/od/collegeprofiles/p/BrynMawr.htm [accessed April 30, 2015].

39. Helen L. Horowitz, Alma Mater: Design and Experience in the Women's Colleges, (Amherst: University of Massachusetts Press, 1993).

40. Margaret Nash and Lisa Romero, "Citizenship for the College Girl," Teacher's College Record, vol. 114. No. 2 (2012):17.

41. National Center for Educational Statistics, "Fast Facts," Digest of Educational Statistics, (2013):Table 21.

42. No author, "Top 10 Women's College Majors," Forbes, (March 2, 2010):4.

43. U.S. Department of Education, National Center for Educational Statistics. (2013) Introduction and Chapter Two.

44. http://elementaryeducation.buffalostate.edu/childhood-education-grades-1–6–bs-0 [accessed April 30, 2015].

45. National Center for Educational Statistics, "Fast Facts," Digest of Educational Statistics, (2013):Table 23.

46. John W. Curtis and Saranna Thornton, "Here's the News: The annual report on the economic status of the profession," University Faculty, (March-April 2013).

47. Daniel deVise, "More Women Than Men Got PhDs Last Year," http://www.washingtonpost.com/wp-dyn/content/article/2010/09/13/AR2010091306555.html [accessed April 30, 2015].

48. Harvard Law School, "2014–2015 Course and Schedule Updates", http://hls.harvard.edu/dept/academics/curriculum/course-and-schedule-updates/, [accessed April 30, 2015].

49. National Association of Women Lawyers, Report of the Sixth Annual National Survey on Retention and Promotion of Women in Law Firms. (October 2011).

50. Bureau OF Labor Statistics, Current Population Survey, "Median Weekly Earnings of Full time Wage and Salary Workers by Detailed Occupation and Sex," Annual Average (2013).

51. Bureau of Labor Statistics, Employed Persons by Occupation, Sex and Race, (2013).

52. David Lat, "How Did the Law School Class Of 2013 Do In The Job Market?" Above the Law, (June 20, 2014):1.

53. Catalyst: "Catalyst Quck Take: Women in Law in the United States," (New York: Catalyst, 2013).

54. No author, "Sandra Day O'Connor," Bio. A&E Television Network, 2014.

55. Jeffrey Tobin, The Nine: Inside the Secret World of the Supreme Court, (New York: Doubleday,2007):82.

56. Meg Greene, Sonia Sotomayor: A Biography. (New York: Greenwood Publishers, 2012).

57. No author, "Elena Kagan: Associate Justice, Supreme Court" The Wall Street Journal, (August 4, 2014):1.

58. National Center for Educational Statistics, Digest of Educational Statistics, (2013):Table 348.

59. Renee Klahr, "College Magazine's Top Ten Journalism Schools," College Magazine, (March 12, 2012):1.

60. https://catalog.ufl.edu/ugrad/current/journalism/majors/journalism.aspx, [accessed April 30, 2015].

61. Bureau of Labor Ststistics.

62. Eric Brown, "What's Next for Jill Abramson's T Tattoo?" International Business Times, (May14, 2014):1.

63. No author, "Biograph: Donna Byrd," History Makers, January 31, 2014):1.

64. Jonathan Pitts, "Right at Home," The Baltimore Sun, (March 9, 2008):E1.

65. No author, "Gail Collins," The New York Times (July 18, 2007):1.,

66. David T. Courtwright, No Right Turn: Conservative Politics in a Liberal America, Cambridge, MA (Harvard University Press, 2010):230.

67. Bureau of Labor Statistics, Tables 619 and 643.

68. "Katherine Ann Couric," The Biography .com Website, http://www.biography.com/people/katie-couric-9542060, [accessed April 30, 2015].

69. Dennis La Beau, Editor, Theater, Film and Television Biographies, (Detroit: Gale Research Co. Index Series, (2013).

70. Brandon Kirby, "Pamela Silva Conde", Hollywood Reporter, (September 20, 2012).

71. Ernest V. Hollis and Alice A. Taylor, Social Work Education in the United States, (New York: Columbia University Press, 1951):9.

72. Grace Khonou, "Social Work is Women's Work," The Social Work Practit0iner, vol. 24, no.1, (2012).

73. Bureau of Labor Statistics, "Labor Force Statistics from the Current Population Survey," Table 11.

Chapter Three

Achieving Women, Their Careers and Their Families

I

In view of the ever increasing number of women who earn as much or more than their husbands, it is remarkable that women who have demonstrated considerable ambition and unusual achievements are sought-after marriage prospects among men with similar drives. Men who have reached financial and/or educational success are interested in finding women with similar ambitions. While previous generations saw men marrying women who were sexually attractive, looked beautiful, and knew how to cook, 21st century high achieving men look for similar women.

More recently, men have shown an interest in women who earn as much or more than they do. This is true of 20% of men. Men in the 21st century are often relieved to find that they will not have to be the sole breadwinner once married and that a woman in whom they are interested can earn as much or more than they.[1]

Moreover, the view that poverty is mostly feminized is being challenged by the evidence that in 2014 men have fallen on hard times, even as women's income and labor force participation has increased since the 1970's. Thus, the median income for men fell by 19% between 1970 and 2014, with those with just a high school diploma losing 41% of earnings. At the end of the recession of 2010–2014, men recovered only 75% of work they once held, while women regained all of the losses they endured during that period. This happened because women gained a good number of high skilled jobs but hardly participated in low skilled jobs. Men lost numerous middle skilled jobs and increased their employment in low skilled jobs.[2]

In 2014, millions of American men are faced with working conditions which were heretofore characteristics of women's lives, I.e. low wages, part time work, temporary jobs, few benefits and repeated joblessness. Another major change in the status-role of men in the second decade of the 21st century is that more and more men are single fathers who have to find child care opportunities and/or work reduced hours, as they no longer have a full time wife/mother to rely on, as was true for so many years in the past. In short, there are now many more father-only families without a mother to play the traditional maternal role.[3]

II

One of the latest features of American family life may be labeled "the blended family." These families consist sixty-five percent of remarriages who bring children from a previous marriage into the new relationship. These "blended" families usually have more children than nuclear families, as mothers and fathers must now pay attention to several additional children to the dismay of one or two of their own. Children want their biological parent to spend time with them and not "the other." The children of blended families are also more likely to fight and suffer sibling rivalry than is common among biological siblings. In addition, "blended" children suffer identity confusion.[4]

An example of identity confusion may be found in the life of President Bill Clinton, whose father, William Jefferson Blythe Jr., died in an auto accident when before Bill was born and named William Jefferson Blythe III. His mother married a man named Clinton, who later adopted him. In school, other children called him Clinton because his mother had that name. Therefore he finally called himself Clinton, because he sought to escape the identity confusion which greatly disturbed him.[5]

Because blended families tend to have large numbers of children, the size of the family creates financial problems. The average cost of raising a child to age eighteen before paying for college has now (2014) been estimated at $245,000. This has become true as food prices have risen 13% since 2004. The U.S. Department of Agriculture has published these expenditures, included in the $245,000. Housing and Transportation, $107,970; Child Care and Education, $44,400; Food 39,000; Clothing and Miscellaneous, $33,780; Health Care, $20,130.[6]

Although blended families as well as a number of other arrangements which deviate from the traditional family are widespread, a large number of Americans still marry one another, as the desire to marry remains very important. However, one of the major changes in marriage patterns at the beginning of the 21st century is the increase in the age of marriage by women. Looking back to 1890, we find that the median age for marriage for men was twenty-six and for women twenty-two. After World War II, the age at marriage fell considerably, to twenty-three for men and twenty for women. Then, during the 1960's- the median age at marriage began to climb. In 2013 the median age of marriage for men became twenty-nine and twenty-seven for women.[7]*

According to Andrew J. Cherlin, prior to the 1960's, the majority of single women and men lived at home with their parents and generally abstained from sexual intercourse. Most singles were employed and therefore turned over a good part of their pay to their parents. Not many went to college and only one in sixteen had a college degree.. One third of adults in their twenties had graduated from high school.[8]

Now (2015), single adults are most likely living in their own apartments. These young adults spend their money on themselves. Five out of six have finished high school and one third have completed college. The vast majority have regular sexual intercourse for five years before marriage, as one half live with someone of the opposite sex. This is labeled cohabitation and serves some as a trial marriage while others engage in a series of such arrangements. Of these, one half end within a year by reason of marriage or because of a breakup.[9]

At the second decade of the 21st century, a considerable number of singe women have children. In 1950, only four percent of unmarried women had children. This had risen to eleven percent in 1970 and reached 28 percent in 1990. In 2003, thirty percent of all American births were by unmarried women. This statistic reached forty percent in 2012. The Centers for Disease Control reported that in 2011 U.S. births were 3,953,593, which was 45,703 less than in 2010, as the general fertility rate of 63.3 per thousand declined to the lowest ever recorded in the United States.[10]*

Divorce has also increased since the beginning of the 20th century. At that time, ten percent of marriages ended in divorce. One third of marriages beginning in 1950 ended in divorce, rising to about 48%

within twenty years for marriages begun in 1990. Thirty years after the beginning of a marriage, divorce reaches about fifty percent.

As the number of births to unmarried and divorced women increased, the number of children living with two biological parents decreased. In 1970, ninety percent of children lived with two parents. In 2009, only 69% of children lived in such a family.[11]

After the 1960's, more and more Americans remained single until the mid-twenties and into the thirties. Some finished college and started careers before marrying, and most married women worked for pay. Unmarried mothers became less stigmatized as the birth rate declined precipitously. Divorce rates rose to fifty percent but declined by ten percent thereafter, as more and more singles lived together without marriage.

This effort to live without the burden of conventional obligations is rooted in the industrial revolution beginning in this country in the middle to the nineteenth century. As factories grew and more and more Americans left the farms and the close-knit farm families for the industrial cities, men and later women left the home to work elsewhere. The family shrank as birthrates declined and the nuclear family became the norm. That in turn liberated men and later women from having to employ all their resources in favor of the family. Men, and later women, met a great number of people at work who were not known to their spouses. This led to social distance between spouses and family members and the breadwinners. In addition, the invention of the automobile made mobility possible, so that many a man or other family member could conduct friendships and even adultery without being recognized or penalized at home. Gradually the bonds of religion and public opinion loosened, and many an adult decided that "till death do us part" is not for them. Moreover, many relatives moved out of the county or state of their birth and settled many miles away from their birthplace. In this new environment, many a woman or man associated with people totally different from those at home, as religious, cultural, and racial intermarriage or cohabitation increased.

III

Biology determines that humans shall reproduce themselves, thereby guaranteeing the perpetuation of human life on this earth. Culture, or the manmade environment, determines the manner in which sexual reproduction shall be achieved. The intergenerational process whereby men accost women and vice versa is enculturated and reflects beliefs about gender and sex as understood and valued at different times and places. Prior to the 21st century and most certainly before 1965, women and men relied mainly on introductions furnished by friends and relatives or by joining voluntary organizations such as religious communities, recreational facilities, and/or social clubs.

Those who met in this manner would go to dinner, for which the gentleman paid. Men had to drive a car to impress women. Men who had no car or a poor model would rent a car for the evening, even as women paid for a "hair-do" and a new dress. Several such dates either led to abandonment or to romance, followed by a wedding and the mandatory 3.1 children. In those years, women would wait by the 'phone for calls from men, as it was "taboo" for women to initiate dating. Women and men who are of dating age in 2015 no doubt find the foregoing brief description of dating as antiquated as a used Studebaker car. It just isn't done that way anymore. Instead, in the 21st century, women are on an equal footing with men, as both sexes take advantage of several new techniques of dating in vogue in the new century, thereby insuring the production of the next generation. One of these is called "speed dating." This method of meeting the opposite sex consists of paying the hosting company for the opportunity to meet eight people for eight minutes each. Those who seek to meet one of the eight participants again have the option of exchanging telephone numbers or email addresses. A more extreme form of "speed dating" is "eye gazing." This consists of men and women sitting across from each other and looking into each other's eyes. Evidently these forms of meeting the opposite sex have been successful, since their attendance is ever increasing. [12]

Speed dating was invented by Rabbi Yaacov Deyo of Los Angeles. In 1998 he wanted to give Jewish singles an opportunity to meet others of their faith. That idea has spread across the United States and other countries, so that commercial entrepreneurs are organizing dating parlors in every American community. Couples pay a fee for meeting a potential date, to whom they talk for no more than eight minutes. Each man then moves until he has sat across from all women then participating. Then each participant states on a questionnaire which person they would like to meet again. Matching participants are provided with contact information by the host for further contact. Women are more anxious than men to find a committed relationship in speed dating as well as in all kinds of dating. Scientists assume that women are more cautious than men in seeking a mate because they produce children, whose support needs commitment from men as well as women. This caution allows women an opportunity to discard risky relationships and so-called "losers." Men are mainly interested in women's looks and sexual potential. Only after finding these qualities of interest will most men deal with other issues such as personality, education, family, etc. [13]

Another means of dating in the 21st century is online dating. Numerous companies have developed dating services online, which charge participants for their services. Many of these online websites are devoted to one ethnic group, such as JDate, which seeks Jewish participants, or Christian Dating, or dating services devoted to single parents or to senior citizens. Participants describe themselves, which leads to much dishonesty and disappointment on first meeting many of those who have used the service. It is evidently tempting to exaggerate one's background and brag about achievements while posting pictures so arranged as to make the subject gorgeous and/or handsome beyond reality. Some young people have resorted to "sexting," which consists of sending pictures of the subject in the nude. This method of meeting others is often very disappointing, as the difference between reality and online communications is enhanced by the imagination and unrealistic expectations. [14]

Yet another means of meeting the opposite sex is "cybersex." This is also called "virtual adultery," in that participants enter "chat rooms," which are areas in a website allowing participants to talk to each other anonymously. Such talk can lead to virtual sexual encounters and cause the subjects to decide to get together. People affected by this interest will sit at the computer for hours, "texting" numerous potential sex partners while ignoring their normal responsibilities. Some participants in this obsession have been divorced by their current spouses, who view that behavior as real adultery. [15]

IV

When Betty Friedan published *The Feminine Mystique* in 1963, she created a true revolution in the American family, as women recognized in that book their widespread unhappiness with the traditional roles assigned to them. That role was that of housewife and mother, without any other kind of fulfillment either professionally or financially. At that time, many young women dropped out of school early for fear they could not attract a husband if they were "too educated." Friedan proposed that women have the same right as men to earn money, follow a career, and engage in politics. Friedan attacked the old fashioned ideas of Sigmund Freud, who viewed women as childlike imbeciles and assigned them passive roles supported by the functionalists who were told they must do nothing but housework lest they upset the balance of social life. She showed that many so called "leaders" in America believed and taught that too much education would lead to a decline in femininity. Friedan then attacked the inequality inherent in lower pay for women at work and the large scale dismissal of women from industrial jobs after the end of World War Two. Friedan then showed that many women filled their time with housework even if they could find time to do other things, because they believed that housework was their only role. According to Friedan, many mothers exhibited their dissatisfaction to their children, who in turn were also dissatisfied with their role in life. She concluded her book with the insistence that women as well as men need to work in useful, interesting, and meaningful occupations. The book develops several suggestions which can help women realize their potential in a manner which has finally come true in the 21st century.

The outcome of this revolutionary book and its approach to feminist liberation was not only the entrance of women into the work world but also the profound changes in family life which have become most manifest during the second decade of the twenty-first century. This means that women have largely freed themselves from "the problem that has no name," as Friedan called it, and have found new ways of gaining access to the male sex and new ways of living together and founding families by means not known in any previous generation.[16]

Whatever means may be used to found an American family in the 21st century, it is evident that living together with an adult of the opposite sex and such children as may result has different dynamics than was customary in all centuries in the United States prior to the gender revolution of the 1960's.

For many years it was assumed that the nuclear family consisting of husband, wife, and children, was an arrangement that was believed to be a biological condition unalterable and permanent. The nuclear family was the norm, the expected behavior of adults, so that any differences were labeled "disorganization." Even the agricultural family, which dominated the years prior to the industrial revolution and included grandparents and other relatives, was nevertheless constructed on the principal that husband, wife, and children were a divine prerequisite to any sexual union and "the building block of society." Family life was considered "women's sphere" while men's sphere was public life. Therefore men, but not women, voted and men, but not women, worked for money outside the home.[17]

Those who supported these views believed that differences could not be tolerated, because different modes of living together seemed to them disorganized attacks on their future and their security. It seemed that American society needed to conserve the accustomed family arrangements lest everything else fall apart. This conservative view assumed that the division of labor based on gender needed to be preserved and that this division of labor between women and men was unalterable, permanent, and final.

Since 1990, a major shift has occurred in the structures of the American family. Now some homosexual couples marry each other in same sex marriages, which have been approved and made legal in sixteen states as of September 2014. On May 17, 2004, Massachusetts was first to accept same sex marriage and make it legal. Massachusetts was followed by Connecticut, Iowa, Vermont,

New Hampshire, New York, Washington, Maine, Maryland, Delaware, Rhode Island, California, Minnesota, Illinois, New Jersey and Hawaii.

The consequences of promoting same sex marriages became visible almost immediately after that social movement succeeded in gaining widespread support. The first of these unanticipated consequences are the effects these arrangements have for children of such unions. Girls who see only women at home after spending the day at school with only female teachers cannot relate well to men, as they have never experienced the presence of a man. This is particularly true of young children, whose grade school teachers are usually women only. It is also reasonable to hold that children need mothers and all that mothering represents. The counter argument must be that children do not need mothers because mothers are obsolete and unnecessary. Likewise, fathers are needed to give children the support fathers can provide and to give children a male role model so that they can understand that there are two genders in this world. The counter argument would have to be that nobody needs a father and that fathers are of no use to children.

The view that an intact family is best suited to meet the needs of children is countered by the view that an intact family is harmful to children. In fact, both mothers and fathers have a biological connection to their children which homosexual adoption cannot replace. Moreover, children of homosexual couples, like children of divorce, feel deprived when meeting other children in school who have two parents of both sexes. Children wonder why they have no father or no mother. Children also learn from their married parents how to conduct their own marriage once they are adults. There is considerable evidence that children raised by same sex partners develop sexual disorders, in that they cannot relate to the opposite sex in a normal fashion. Marriage has always been viewed as having a procreative purpose. Widespread same sex marriage would lead to the utter decimation of humanity, which may well be a good idea.*

There are more arguments against same sex marriages which concern the financial consequences for taxpayers. For homosexual couples, the advantages of marriage include the right to file a joint income tax return, thereby reducing taxes for both spouses in some cases, inheriting a share of the spouse's estate, receiving Social Security, Medicare and disability benefits, receiving public assistance benefits, gaining insurance benefits through the spouse's employer, receiving equal property rights on divorce, receiving spousal maintenance payments upon separation or divorce, and many more benefits not listed here.

These advantages will of course attract others seeking such benefits for polygamous couples or for people who seek to marry their own children or people who wish to marry a dog or other animal or people who seek to marry an inanimate object like their car.[18]

V

It is evident that female headed households are generally poorer and have fewer financial assets than male headed households. The principal reason for this is not only that women have traditionally earned less than men, but also because many young women who have children do not have the education nor the work experience needed to earn a sufficient income for supporting an entire family. Of course, those who have only one child have less of a financial burden than those with multiple children. Yet even those households are not doing very well. The Census Bureau has published statistics concerning the gender and size of household in 2013. This indicates that there were in that year 15,469,000 female headed American households out of a total of 122,459,000 households. [19]

In 1996, during the Clinton Administration, the federal government enacted the Personal Responsibility and Work Opportunity and Reconciliation Act. This law was designed to tie work availability to the receipt of welfare payments, with the provision that cash assistance was to be limited to two years without engaging in work, and that the lifetime limit of receiving such assistance is five years. This measure is called Temporary Assistance to Needy Families. The consequences of this change from the previous Aid To Families with Dependent Children law was at once felt mostly by female headed families. [20]

Poor families, and particularly female headed families, seldom accumulate wealth because they cannot save anything. Indeed, some wealth is developed by reason of home ownership. However, that is hardly useful in developing a source of cash with which to invest in real estate or in stocks and bonds. As a result, it has been estimated that 63% of female headed households are asset poor. [21]

In the course of a lifetime, those who can do so will accumulate assets in their youth and middle age which they can then use when they are old. This means that depending on the time of any life cycle, the assets of any individual are determined by his age and his economic and demographic condition. As income increases, so do assets. However, households earning less than $20,000 have assets of only $2,000, while those whose income is in the vicinity of $100,000 have a net worth of $235,000. Therefore, households in the lowest quartile of income earn so little that they cannot live more than a few days off their accumulated assets. [22]

The welfare laws require that the recipients seek work. Their income from work is then deducted from their welfare checks. Hence, as their income increases, the welfare payments decrease. Furthermore, it is inadvisable for a welfare recipient to save, for those who do so will soon find that they are ineligible for welfare because their assets are too large. This means that the government actually promotes dependency and undermines independence. [23]

It is no secret that the net worth of female headed households is less than that in which men participate in the support of the family. Any comparison of female headed households to any other type of family arrangement indicates that female headed households have had the lowest income and the lowest assets of any other type of family arrangement. This feature is supported by the evidence that the level of education and the level of labor force participation is lower among females who head a household than among women living in a household including a man.[24]

Because the raising of children is expensive and because more women can make independent decisions concerning their reproductive activities, the American birth rate has fallen from 14.7 in 2000 to 12.7 in 2013. Earlier birth rates were far higher. In 1910 the American birth rate was 30.1. It fell to 23.7 in 1960 and declined to 16.7 in 1990. The birthrate is the number of children born per 1,000 people. Likewise the fertility rate, I.e. the number of births per 1,000 women ages 10–44, has reached a record low in the United States, from 64.1 in 2010 to 63.2 in 2013. This resulted in the births of 3,953,593 children in the United States in 2013, down from four million or more in previous years.[25]

It is significant that the birthrates of educated women are higher than those with little education. The birthrate of women with professional degrees or doctorates is 66 per 1,000 women. Those who hold a bachelor's degree display a birth rate of 56.2, those with a high school diploma but no college have a birth rate of 57.7 and those with no high school diploma had a birth rate in 2013 of 46.8.[26]

This indicates that women who with higher education earn more than those with less education and can therefore afford more children. Moreover, educated women are more likely to have educated male partners who also earn more than the average. It is of course evident that highly educated women and men are a minority of Americans and therefore do not have a major impact on the birth rate or the fertility rate.

A distinction must be made between income and assets, a difference which impacts women and children in a female headed household. Assets are holdings which bring security to a family in face of low earnings or layoffs or other reasons for unemployment such as illness. Someone who owns a house or a car and does not need to make payments on these belongings is far better off than those who need to worry about the mortgage and the "repo" man.[27]

Assets induce people to have a future orientation, in that the possibilities of gaining advantages later are inducements to graduate from high school or enter college or start a business or invest in possible economic gains. Children's educational attainment is colored by the attitude of parents and that attitude is largely influenced by the possession of assets or by poverty. A low level of economic resources translates into anxiety and behavior which is transmitted to children. In short, it is well known that parental income is related to children's wellbeing.[28]

There is a good deal of evidence that parental income is positively related to years of formal schooling, so that the children of wealthy people have a better chance of attending medical school or law school or earning a degree from a prestigious university than is true of those who have little income and few assets. In fact, a considerable number of children of high earning parents attend elite schools which one or both parents can afford, a practice which is also true of medical schools, often attended by children of doctors, or business schools, attended by the children of successful women and men in the business world.[29]

All of this indicates that the children of high earning women gain advantages over life which mothers who earn little money cannot provide, so that it is no exaggeration to hold the view that the rich get richer and that therefore there is an untitled American aristocracy. It It has also been found that children of homeowners are less likely to drop out of school as compared to renters. Evidently, those who achieve enough to own a home are also more likely to expect their children to finish high school and go on to college. Likewise, those who are themselves educated are more likely to own a home than those who earn too little to become homeowners because they do not have a high school diploma or a college degree.[30]

Achieving women are attracting men. According to Terrence Real, a psychologist and author, high achieving men seek women who are also achievers. This is also true of divorced men seeking a second marriage with a high earning and high achieving woman. These men want impressive women in the office so that women with degrees "count for more than Miss America."[31]

VI

Achieving women as well as achieving men are heavily influenced by the expectations of parents and teachers. These expectations are in turn influenced by the expectations of the culture in which women and men grow up and become socialized. Traditionally, girls were led to believe that they were not as capable as boys in dealing with mathematics as taught in American schools. This belief was delivered to girls above the grade school level and had debilitating consequences for women, as failure to master mathematics excluded women from the highest paying jobs in industry and commerce.

We have already seen that the most highly paid American women have degrees in engineering, which requires a good deal of mathematical training. Therefore it is reasonable to speculate that women who have engineering degrees came from families who expected them to be competent in mathematics.[32]

Children are not only subject to school learning but also learn by observation. Therefore the children of achieving mothers and fathers are more likely to become achievers as well. For girls, this means that high achieving mothers can become their role models, so that they also achieve. Nevertheless there are a number of achieving women whose mothers were housewives. This means that verbal expectations by mothers can be very effective in promoting the ambitions of their daughters. Furthermore, some girls will view their father as their role model and become successful by that gendered route.

Exceptionally successful people, whether male or female, have a family background which had considerable influence on their future development because that is true of all. It is therefore true of high achieving women and is reflected in their achievements in their early years. One of these is Marissa Mayer, the president of Yahoo. She is the daughter of Margaret Mayer and Michael Mayer of Wausau, Wisconsin, where she grew up. Her parents, of Finnish descent, were both professionals and college graduates. Her mother was an art teacher and her father an environmental engineer. As a child she was excessively shy until she joined the Brownies, a Girl Scout group, and later took piano and dancing lessons. She became so proficient at dancing that she was elected into membership on a precision dance team. She became president of her high school class, president of the Spanish club, captain of the debate team, and captain of the pompom squad. She was selected by then governor of Wisconsin, Tommy Thompson, to the National Youth Science Camp in West Virginia.

When she entered Stanford University, Mayer intended to become a pediatric neurosurgeon, and therefore took "pre-med" classes. Later she decided to major in symbolic systems and also danced the "Nutcracker Ballet." She participated in parliamentary debates and volunteered to bring computer science education to Bermuda. She also volunteered at a children's hospital. Later she taught classes at Stanford in symbolic systems and then graduated with an honors B.S. in 1997 and an M.S. in 1999. Her specialization was in artificial intelligence. She was granted a doctorate from the Illinois Institute of Technology, leading to fourteen job offers, including a teaching job at Carnegie Mellon University. She decided to join Google, where she became the first female engineer. There she became vice president in charge of numerous projects until she was appointed president of Yahoo in 2012. Thereafter Mayer was repeatedly listed as "Woman of the Year" and "Most Powerful Woman in America" under age forty. She was thirty-three at that time. She is married to Zachary Bogue, with whom she has a son Macallister. A Lutheran, she names her priorities, "God, family, and Yahoo".[33]

The family of Margaret Whitman may well be regarded as a member of The Protestant Establishment, as E. Digby Baltzell called them.[34]

Margaret Whitman's father was Hendricks Hallett Whitman, a Wall Street financial advisor and business man. He was a descendant of Elnathan Whitman (1700–1777), who had been pastor of the second church of Christ in Hartford, Connecticut, and one of the founders of Yale University.

In addition to having a great deal of wealth and belonging to a "prominent" family, Whitman was endowed with ambition and intelligence. She graduated from high school in three years, then enrolled at Princeton University, and earned a Harvard MBA in 1978. She then continued her career at Proctor and Gamble and moved to San Francisco with her husband, neurosurgeon Griff

Harsh, with whom she has two sons. There she worked for Mitt Romney until she became CEO of eBay.

In 2009, Whitman ran for governor of California as Republican candidate but lost to Democrat Jerry Brown. Then, in September of 2011, she became CEO of Hewlett-Packard, a computer giant.[35]

Sharon Jester Turney is president of "Victoria's Secret," a $6.1 billion company. She was born is a small Oklahoma town. Her father was a cattle rancher and her mother a nutritionist. She graduated with a degree in business education, and then married Charles Turney, with whom she has one son.

She began her career as a buyer for Foley's department store in Houston, Texas, and then joined Neiman Marcus, where she became executive vice president and general merchandise manager, later to become president of NM's catalogue division. In 2000, she was appointed president of the Victoria's Secret catalog division, and in 2006 was promoted to president and CEO. In 2014 Turney was one of only two women included in "America's Favorite Bosses" list. In 2005 she received the Dr. Catherine White Achievement Award from Heart Share Human Services in New York City, and in 2009 she was awarded the H.U.G. award from the Intimate Apparel Square Club in honor of having raised funds for pediatric charities. In 2013 she was inducted into the Hall of Fame by the University of Oklahoma business department.

Turney is a member of the board of Nationwide Children's Hospital and the Columbia Coalition against Family Violence. [36]

Virginia Rometty is chairman and CEO of IBM, earning $1.5 million a year. Before becoming CEO, she was senior vice president at IBM. She has been named to Fortune magazine's "50 Most Powerful Women in Business" for several years and in 2014 included in "World's 100 Most Powerful Women." She received similar ratings in Time and Bloomberg's magazines.

Rommety graduated with a degree in electrical engineering from Northwestern University in 1979 with high honors. She then went to work for General Motors and in 1981 joined IBM as a systems engineer. In 2009 she became senior vice president for sales and marketing. In that capacity, she was instrumental in expanding IBM's business into a number of advanced and newly developed areas. When the previous chairman retired, Rommety was appointed to also assume that position. She is also a member of numerous boards of charitable organizations as well as the board of trustees of Northwestern University.

Married to Mark Anthony Rommety, she was born Virginia Marie Nicosia in Chicago in 1957. She has no children. Raised by a single mother, she is the eldest of four siblings. Her brother and her two sisters all achieved extraordinary success in the business world.[37]

These are a sample of some women who have achieved a great deal in the American world of business and industry. Those who have done so appear to have a mindset which promotes their interests and is related to their experiences in a competitive environment. Like high achievers among men, achieving women believe that they have to do things perfectly. This is of course not possible, alone because the word "perfect" is ambiguous and nearly without meaning. Women who seek perfection cannot win, since perfect is a subjective opinion with many definitions. High achievers are generally of the view that they can manage everything they believe they should do. This can be disastrous because such a belief is open ended because no one can say what doing it all really means. Because high achievements involve stress, it is common for high achievers to suffer from physical symptoms such as headaches and muscle spasms and digestive issues. One of the most common beliefs among high achievers is the notion that she must prove herself to all her coworkers. Many high achievers are afraid they are not accepted everywhere and therefore load themselves with unattainable burdens. Women who work stressful and demanding jobs will nevertheless believe that they must also cook great meals, keep a spotless house, and be great at "romance." This attitude is self-defeating, because nothing can ever prove that the achiever has ever attained all of these goals.[38]

Many high achievers cannot relax. They believe that relaxation is a reward eventually to be enjoyed but always out of reach because there is always more to do, so that work is never done. These achievers criticize themselves, believing that they should do more each day that what has been done. Added to this belief is the view that one must be a people pleaser and that one must do everything oneself. It may well be that some can overcome these stressors. However, the evidence is that that high achievers are generally plagued by these self-created sources of anxiety.

The Academy of Women Achievers is located in Boston, Massachusetts, and "celebrates women who have demonstrated outstanding leadership and achievement in their professional and civic lives." Since 1995, the academy has named a few women "who have championed gender equality." Among these women are Stephanie Lovell, Dianne Phillips, Helene Solomon, and Evelyn Murphy, the last of whom was granted the "lifetime achievement award" in 2014.

Murphy is the author of Getting Even: Why Women Don't Get Paid Like Men and What To Do About It. She is the founding president of WAGE, a national organization seeking to eliminate the gender wage gap. Murphy is the first woman to have been elected Lieutenant Governor of Massachusetts, after first serving as Secretary of Economic Affairs.

Evelyn Murphy holds a B.A. degree in mathematics from Duke University, an M.A. degree in economics from Columbia University, and a Ph.D. degree in economics also from Duke. She has been a visiting fellow at Harvard University and at Brandeis University and has received over one hundred awards. She has run the Boston Marathon five times.

Dr. Murphy was elected to the boards of directors of a number of companies. Including Bay State HMO, Blue Cross and Blue Shield, the Shawmut National Bank, and the Fleet National Bank.

Murphy is also active on the boards of a number of civic organizations.[39]

At a recent panel discussion at the Wharton School of Business at the University of Pennsylvania, four female executives with families described their personal lives. Included were Aileen Sands, vice president of global investment banking at Chase Securities, Kara Gruver, vice president at Bain & Co., Peggy Maher, vice president at American Express, and Tracy Ramirez, manager at Merck (Pharmaceuticals).

All four women expressed the need for support from home. They agreed that a husband with a flexible schedule is most important when they have to balance job responsibilities with family needs. Sands' husband is a "stay at home dad," so that her marriage is a role reversal difficult for any man to accept. Ramirez put her child in full time daycare; her husband picks up the child because she is too busy even late in the afternoon to do so. Maher and husband both work for American Express. They employ a full time nanny.

Gruver is married to a cardiologist who is also unable to concentrate much on family. They claim to take turns every year concentrating on their children. Although none of the panelists said so explicitly, it is evident that children are in their way as they pursue high paying careers.

Because children and career clash inevitably, the advance of women into leadership positions in business will always create tensions which cannot be avoided no matter whether a nanny is employed, the husband is a stay-at-home, or children are sent to full time nurseries. This dilemma also faces elected officials, as we will see in the next chapter.[40]

Summary

Women are gaining financially and professionally, even as many men now face the same economic job problems that were traditionally known only to women.

Another great change in male-female relations is the blended family, which consists of two formerly married, divorced, and now remarried couples with children. In addition, single women and some single men with children have become commonplace in America.

Dating has also changed a great deal, as online dating, speed dating, and cybersex have taken the place of the former means of meeting the opposite sex.

All this has had a profound effect on income and wealth, as more and more women produce higher and higher incomes, while many men fall behind. These advances are not without costs, as mothers of small children with major work responsibilities are subject to all kinds of emotional and even physical consequences of their anomic lives.

Notes

1. Stephanie Coontz, "How Can We Help Men? By Helping Women" The New York Times, (January 11, 2014):1–5.

2. Ibid.

3. Ibid:6.

4. Jeanette Lofas, Step-Parenting. (New York: Kensington Publishing Co. 2004):34.

5. David Maraniss, First in His Class: A Biography of Bill Clinton, New York: Touchstone Press, (1995):24–29.

6. U.S. Department of Agriculture, Expenditure on Children by Families, (Washington, DC, 2013).

7. Eleanor Barkhorn, Getting Married Later Is Great for College-Educated Women, The Atlantic, (March 15, 2013):74.

8. U.S. Bureau of the Census, "Percentage of People 25 Years Old and Over Who Have Completed High School or College," (June 24, 2004):Table A2.

9. Larry L. Bumpass and Hsien-Hen Lu, "Trends in Co-habitation and Implication for Children," Population Studies, vo.54, (2000):29–41.

* The author is indebted to Professor Andrew J. Cherlin, whose excellent article "American Marriage in the 21st Century," is the basis for this discussion.

10. Daniel Greenfield, "Welfare State Watch: 40% of Babies born to Unmarried Mothers." Front Page Magazine.

11. Matthew Bramlett, et.al., Cohabitation, Marriage, Divorce and Remarriage in the United States, vol.22, no.2 (U.S. National Center for Health Statistics, 2002).

*The foregoing statistics were collected by Andrew Cherlin of Johns Hopkins University.

12. Bruce Bower, "The Dating Go Round," Science News, (February 14, 2009):22–23.

13. Eli Finkel and Paul Eastwick, "Speed Dating," Current Direction in Psychological Science, vol.17, no.3 (June 2008):193–197.

14. Alex Williams, "The End of Courtship," The New York Times, (January 30, 2013):ST1.

15. Albert Mohler, "Virtual Adultery-The Emergence of Cyber Sinning," The Sydney Morning Herald, (August 22, 2005):1.

16. Betty Friedan, The Feminine Mystique. (New York: W.W. Norton & Co. 1963).

17. Nancy Klingsbury and John Scanzoni, "Structural Functionalism." In: Sourcebook of Family Theories, William J. Doherty, Editor (New York: Plenum Press, 1993)

18. The Family Research Council, http://www.frc.org, [accessed May 11. 2015].

19. U.S. Department of Labor, Bureau of the Census, "Households by type and tenure of householder," (2013):Table H1.

20. Ralph G. Hubbard, "The Second Term Economy," The Wall Street Journal, (November 17,2004):A18.

21. Robert Haveman and Barbara Wolfe, "Where Are the Asset Poor?" Madison, Wisconsin: Robert M. La Follette School of Public Affairs. (1993–1998):2000.

22. Edward N. Wolff, "Recent Trends in the Size and Distribution of Household Wealth." (Working Paper No. 300). Annandale-on-Hudson, NY: Jerome Levy Economics Institute of Bard College.

23. Elizabeth T. Powers,"Does means testing welfare discourage savings?" Journal of Public Eonomics,vol.68. (1998):33–53.

24. Gary Burtless, "Growing American Inequality: Sources and Remedies," The Brookings Review, vol. 17, no.1:31–35.

25. Brady E. Hamilton et. al. "Annual Summary of Vital Statistics, 2011," Pediatrics, vol.131, no.3 (February 11, 2013).

26. No author, "Birthrate in the United States 2013 by education attainment of mother 24519/statistics.

27. Melvin L. Oliver and Thomas M. Shapiro , Black Wealth, White Wealth: A New Perspective on Racial Inequality, (New York: Routledge, 1995).

28. Jere Cohen, "Parents as educational models and definers," Journal of Marriage and the Family, 49(2):339–51.

29. Susan T. Mayer, What Money Can't Buy: Family Income and Children's Life Chances. (Cambridge, MA: Harvard University Press, 1997).

30. Carol Dwek, et. al., "Sex Differences in Learned Helplessness," Developmental Psychology, vol. 15 (1978):268–276.

31. Deborah Siegel, "The New Trophy Wife," Psychology Today, (January 1, 2004):3.

32. Jacquelynne E. Parsons, "Cognitive Developmental Factors in Emerging Sex Differences in Achievement Related Expectancies," Journal of Social Issues, vol. 32, (1976):47–61.

33. Nicholas Carlson, "The Truth About Marissa Mayer," Business Insider, (August 25, 2013):8.

34. E. Digby Baltzell, The Protestant Establishment, (New York: Random House, 1964).

35. "Meg Whitman," http://www.biography.com/people/meg-whitman-20692533 [accessed May 12, 2015].

36. Rusty Whitman, "NM Direct Taps Turney as President, Chief Exec," Women's Wear Daily, vol 177, no. 54:2.

37. James B. Stewart, "A CEO's Support System," The New York Times, (November 5, 2011).

38. Henry Braiker, "The Type E Woman: How to Overcome the Stress of Being Everything to Everybody," Lincoln, NB: iUniverse, Inc., (2006):206.

39. Women's Media Center. http://www.shesource.org/experts/profile/evelyn-murphy, [accessed May 12, 2015].

40. No author, "Balancing Work and family: Fur Women Executives Speak." Leadership. (May 24, 2000).

Chapter Four

American Women in Politics and Government

I

On January 5, 1925, Nellie T. Ross was inaugurated the first woman ever to be elected to governor of an American state. She was the widow of Wyoming governor William Ross, who had died a few months earlier. She was a "progressive" politician who favored improving the safety of coal miners, protecting women working in industrial jobs, cutting back on child labor, and enforcing the prohibition laws.

She lost the next election but remained in politics when President Franklin Roosevelt named her director of the U.S. mint. She remained in that job for four terms of five years each. She lived to become 101 years old.

The election of Ross in Wyoming was preceded by the passage of a Wyoming law allowing women to vote in state elections as early as 1890. This was unprecedented, except that New Jersey had at one time allowed women to vote only to have that right eliminated shortly thereafter. Federal elections were not open to female votes until 1920.[1]

Miriam Wallace Ferguson was elected governor of Texas after her husband Jim Ferguson was impeached during his second term. She was largely guided by her husband but eventually made her own decisions, such as granting 2,000 pardons to convicted offenders. She served two years of Jim's term, and was re-elected in 1926 but defeated in 1930. She was elected once more, but lost in 1940 at age sixty-five.[2]

The elections of two women governors were indeed revolutionary in the early twentieth century. Although unusual, it became possible because women won the right to vote when Congress and the states passed the 19th Amendment to the U.S. Constitution in 1919 and ratified it in 1920. This amendment was the result of decades of agitation and protest by women seeking to gain a right which is not questioned at the beginning of the 21st century but was vigorously opposed in earlier years.[3]

Shortly before the 2014 November elections, there were only five female governors in the United States. They were the Republicans Nikki Haley of South Carolina, Jan Brewer of Arizona, Susana Martinez of New Mexico ,and Mary Felling of Oklahoma. Maggie Hassan of New Hampshire is the only Democrat on the list.

The first woman elected to the U.S. Senate was Hattie Caraway of Arkansas, who was elected in 1932. Since then, few women have ever been made senators, so that there were a number of years when no woman served in the U.S. Senate. As of 2014, this had changed greatly. There were, at the end of 2014, twenty women in the U.S. Senate. They were Barbara Mikulski, D–MD; Susan

Collins R-ME; Kelly Ayotte, R-NH; Barbara Boxer, D-CA; Maria Cantwell; D-WA; Dianne Feinstein, D-CA; Kirsten Gillibrand D-NY; Kay Hagan, D-NC; Mazie Hironu, D-HI; Amy Klobuchar, D-MN; Mary Landrieu, D-LA; Claire McCaskill, D-MO; Patty Murray, D-WA; Lisa Murkowski R-AK; Jeanne Shaheen, D-NH; Debbi Stabenow, D-Ml; Heidi Heitkamp D-ND; Elizabeth Warren, D-MA; Debbie Fischer, R-NE; Tammy Baldwin, D-WI.

Not all politicians are elected. In fact, the number of politicians who are appointed to public office is far greater than the number elected. Among those who have held prominent appointments are women who have been or are members of the presidents' cabinet. The highest ranking among these women are three who have been Secretary of State, I.e. Madeleine Albright, who was appointed by President Clinton in 1997, Condoleezza Rice, appointed by President George W. Bush in 2005, and Hilary Clinton, appointed by President Barack Obama in 2009.

President Obama also appointed Penny Pritzker Secretary of Commerce. Pritzker has assets of $1.7 billion. She has supported Obama since he ran for senator from Illinois and continued her financial support during both of his campaigns for the presidency. The Pritzker family was instrumental in financing Obama's first election to the Senate from Illinois.[4]

The first woman to hold a cabinet position was Frances Perkins, who was appointed secretary of labor by President Franklin Roosevelt in 1933. Including Perkins, twenty-two women have been appointed cabinet members.[5]

Women have also been appointed ambassadors of the United States to foreign countries. While such ambassadors were at one time experienced foreign service officers, ambassadors are now mostly wealthy contributors to the president's election campaign. This has become true because rich people buy social honors and because the president can deal with foreign governments himself by calling or emailing right from his desk at the White House. In short, ambassador has become mainly a social honor, not very much needed in the electronic world.

An example of such an ambassador is Ambassador to Japan Caroline Kennedy, the daughter of President Jack Kennedy. She was appointed by President Obama in 2013 and promptly confirmed by the U.S. Senate. This is not surprising, since she has assets of $280 million and has therefore been able to contribute considerable sums to the Obama campaigns.[6]

II

One of the most remarkable women to become governor is Nimrata Nikki Randhawa Haley of South Carolina. The daughter of Indian immigrants, she was raised a Sikh. She married Michael Haley in 1996 and converted to Methodist. Although now a Christian, she also attends a Sikh gurdwara. Her husband is a federal employee with whom she has two children.[7]

Haley is the first woman to become governor of South Carolina. A Republican, she graduated from Clemson University with a degree in accounting. Prior to becoming governor, she held a number of voluntary and political offices, including member of the South Carolina House of Representatives. In 2010 she was elected governor.

The governor of New Hampshire is Margaret Wood Hassan. A graduate of Brown University, she also earned a J.D. degree from Northeastern University. She practiced law until she was elected to the New Hampshire State Senate in 2004, and was re-elected until 2010, when she was defeated. In 2012 she was elected governor and was sworn in on January 3, 2013 for a two year term.

Hassan is married to Thomas Hassan, principal of the Phillips Exeter Academy located in Exeter. The Academy is a private school devoted to enrolling the "elite," as described by sociologists as "The Protestant Establishment." She lives there, rather than in the governor's mansion in Concord, with her family, including two children.[8]

The first woman ever elected to the U.S. Senate was Hattie Wyatt Caraway, who filled the vacancy caused by the death of her husband Thaddeus. Rebecca Felton preceded her, but served only one day in 1922 after she was appointed as a reward for a "long career in Georgia politics and journalism."

Since then forty-two more women have been elected to the U.S. Senate. In earlier years, these women were the widows of senators. More recently, female senators won seats on their own, so that twenty women were members of the U.S. Senate in 2014. Included is Dianne Goldman Feinstein of California, who became a U.S. senator in 1992. She had previously been the mayor of San Francisco, a position she literally inherited from George Moscone when Moscone was murdered in his office by Dan White, a former policeman and member of the Board of Supervisors, who also murdered Harvey Milk, a fellow member of that board.[9]

Feinstein was president of the board at the time of these murders and therefore assumed the position of mayor, because the board president was the designated successor to any mayor who could not remain in office until the end of his term.

In 1992 Feinstein won the special election to the U.S. Senate alongside Barbara Boxer, so that since then California has had two female senators.

Feinstein won reelection four times, receiving 7.7 million votes which are the most popular votes in U.S history for any U.S. Senator. Feinstein is chair of the Select Committee on Intelligence, and is the first woman to ever preside over a U.S. presidential inauguration.[10]

Feinstein has been married three times. She divorced her first husband, Jack Berman, and later married neurosurgeon Bertram Feinstein, who died in 1978. Her third husband is investment banker Richard Blum.[11]

Feinstein's wealth has been estimated at $99 million, which are clearly derived from her husband's assets. This considerable wealth is so common among

American senators that the U.S. Senate has often been described as a million-aire's club.[12]

Hillary Rodham Clinton was elected to the U.S. Senate from New York as a Democrat in 2000. She was re-elected in 2006 but resigned in 2009 to accept a position as Secretary of State in the Obama administration. She resigned that post in 2013 in an effort to campaign for President of the United States.

Clinton has a lifelong interest in politics, fostered in part by her husband William Jefferson Blythe Clinton, who held a number of political offices in his home state of Arkansas until he became governor of that state and President of the United States from 1993 to 2001.

Hillary was born in 1947 in a Chicago suburb, Park Ridge. She graduated from Wellesley College in 1969 and then graduated from the Yale Law School in 1973. She entered politics during the Nixon administration and participated as a staff member of the House Judiciary Committee in the impeachment proceedings against Nixon in 1974.

She married Bill Clinton in 1975 and became First Lady of Arkansas from 1979 until 1993, when she became First Lady of the United States until 2001. As First Lady she participated actively in politics, going so far as to develop a universal health insurance plan submitted to Congress. Her plan was not adopted but it gave her an inordinate amount of publicity. She therefore accumulated a following in New York, which led to her election to the U.S. Senate in 2000, so that she assumed that office on January 3, 2001 shortly before she and the President left the White House on January 20 of that year. She is the only "first lady" to hold national office and to serve as Secretary of State.

In 2008 Hillary Clinton attempted to gain the Democrat nomination for President of the United States. There is a possibility that Clinton would have won the primary contest if the votes of Florida and Michigan had been accepted. The Democratic National Committee refused to count the primary votes of these two states because the voting had occurred earlier than the DNC permitted. A compromise at the convention attempted to reconcile the contesting delegates with the result that Obama was nominated. Consequently Obama appointed Hillary Clinton Secretary of State, so that she remained in the public arena.[13]

Another female senator is Debra Strobel Fischer, who was elected Republican Senator from Nebraska and assumed office in January 2013. She defeated Bob Kerrey in the election of November 6, 2012.

Fischer graduated from the University of Nebraska with a degree in education. She is married to a wealthy rancher and began her political career when she won election to the Nebraska legislature in 2004. Re-elected in 2008, she was barred from a third term by Nebraska's law limiting membership in the legislature to two terms.

During her membership in the legislature she did a weekly radio show and also wrote a column printed in a number of Nebraska newspapers. A strong opponent of abortion, she was elected to the senate. She supports the right to own firearms and also supports "right to life" groups. She is also a critic of the Environmental Protection Agency. She pledged to limit herself to two terms in the U.S. Senate and favors a Constitutional amendment imposing term limits on members of Congress.[14]

III

Any discussion of women in politics inevitably leads to a consideration of electing a woman president of the United States. Because other democracies have already elected women to be prime ministers and heads of state, it seems incongruous that the USA, the leading democracy in the world, has not emulated England, Israel, Norway, and others in doing so.

This deficiency may well be alleviated if Hillary Clinton becomes the Democrat candidate for president in 2016. In 2015 she is considered a most probable candidate for the highest office in the land. This appears to be the case because she hinted repeatedly in advance of running that she would seek the Democrat nomination for president in 2016 but also because her experience appears to qualify her to run for that office.

Her visibility allowed her to collect large speaking fees and to campaign unofficially before making a formal announcement of her candidacy.

In view of the 2014 Republican mid-term victory in both the Senate and House, it is possible that Republicans can win the presidency in 2016 if a candidate can be found who can oppose Clinton effectively. It is therefore reasonable to consider whether the Republican Party could find a woman to run for president. Inspection of these election results indicates that only 7% of House Republicans are women, compared to 33% among Democrats.

The possible Republican candidates are Senator Kelly Ayotte, of New Hampshire, Suzanna Martinez, Governor of New Mexico, and possibly the newly elected Republican Senator from Iowa, Joni Ernst. Other than these few women, the Republican Party would have to reach out to a woman not holding political office, such as Carly Fiorina, formerly the president of Hewlett-Packard, who is actively recruiting staff in an effort to attain the Republican nomination in 2016.[15]

Katherine Ann Bailey Hutchinson served in the U.S. Senate from Texas beginning in 1993 until her retirement in 2013. She had been a member of the House of Representatives from 1972 until 1976, when she was appointed to the National Safety Transportation Board. In 1990 she became Texas state treasurer and in 1992 co-chair of the Republican convention. When Lloyd Bentsen resigned from the U.S. Senate in 1993 she filled the unexpired term, and was then elected to the Senate in 1994, 2000, and 2006. She resigned her seat in 2009 in order to run for governor of Texas, a contest she lost to Rick Perry.

Hutchinson is a graduate of the University of Texas School of Law. She has been married twice and has two adopted children. She divorced her first husband

and married Ray Hutchinson, former Republican state chairman and member of the legislature. He died in 2014. She is the stepmother of two children.

Hutchinson was the first woman to represent Texas in the U.S. Senate after receiving more than four million votes. This was in part due to her high visibility, as she had been a political correspondent for KPRC in Houston. Her assets were reported at $6.7 million as of 2014.[16]

Lisa Murkowski was elected to the U.S. Senate from Alaska in 2002 and re-elected in 2004. She filled the unexpired term of her father, Frank H. Murkowski, who resigned his seat. Elected in 2004, she was not re-nominated by the Republican party in 2010 but was elected as a write-in candidate to serve as senator until January 3, 2017. It is extremely difficult to succeed as a write-in candidate. Lisa Murkowski succeeded nevertheless because she had a great deal of experience in other forms of government employment. She had been district attorney in Anchorage from 1980–1989; on the Mayor's Task Force on the Homeless from 1990–1991; Equal Rights Commissioner in Anchorage 1990–1998; and was a Member of the Alaska State House of Representatives between 1999 and 2002. Her husband is Verne Martell, with whom she has two children.[17]

In January of 2014, women comprised 79, or 18%, of members of the House of Representatives of the 113th Congress. There are now, in the next Congress, 100 women for the first time in congressional history. The first woman to ever serve as a Representative was Jeannette Rankin, who was elected in 1917, and as late as 1991 there were only 32 women in Congress.

A number of female representatives have been widows who may be regarded as "place holders," to serve only until the next election could allow a man to run for the ensuing term. However, a few of these women subsequently ran and were elected on their own merit. The most successful example is Margaret Chase Smith of Maine, who served a total of 32 years in both houses and became the first woman to be elected to the House and the Senate.[18]

The first and only female speaker of the House is Nancy Pelosi, who presided over the House from 2000–2010. She represents a California district including San Francisco. The daughter of the former mayor of Baltimore, she has been interested in politics all her life. She married Paul Pelosi, with whom she has five children. The Pelosis have estimated assets worth $17 million.[19]

IV

Although 1992 was labeled "The Year of the Woman," not much changed then concerning the participation of women in politics. In comparison to other Western democracies, American women were then and are now far less likely to be elected or appointed to government positions. As late as 2012, the United States placed in the bottom half of membership in the so-called "lower house," which is the House of Representatives in the United States. That means that the United

States placed 51st among 88 nations, with 17.8% female representation. Since the Congress that was sworn in in 2015 has 100 women in the House, this increase raises the proportion of women in Congress to 23%.

Women constitute more than 40% of members in the parliaments of Sweden, Finland, and South Africa, and Rwanda boasts a female membership of 63.8%.[20]

Approximately 24% of state legislators are women, so that women are decidedly underrepresented at both the national and local levels of American government, as women are 51% of the American population.[21]

That representation is influenced by party politics in that Republican women have had far more difficulty gaining seats in state legislatures than is true of Democrats. In fact, in some states, Republican representation has been reversed as the party has become more conservative. The Democrats have allied themselves more effectively than Republicans with feminist groups and have also recruited numerous working women, leading to the conclusion that there will be more Democrat women available for higher office than is true of Republicans.[22]

There are regional differences concerning female representation in American government. For example, both senators from New Hampshire are women. This is also true of California.

Nevertheless, men are still the considerable majority of elected officials nationally and locally. This is largely true because of tradition, but also because men are more often encouraged by other men to run for office, and party bosses are more likely to promote men rather than women. Moreover, women are less likely to gain the attention of powerful men than is true of men.

The opportunity to run for higher offices is largely dependent on having held a lower office. This means that incumbency determines career politics. Since men are already entrenched in numerous elected offices, they have a better chance than women, who are only beginning to hold an office and therefore are less likely to be experienced office holders. Those who have held a prior elected office are also more likely to win a higher office because they are experienced campaigners and have an entrenched campaign organization. It is of course unfortunate and contrary to democratic principles to find so many career politicians hanging on to membership in state legislatures and in Congress. This was by no means envisioned by the founders of this republic, who believed that elected offices would be open to all citizens and not only a few. Now we also find that many members of Congress, numerous governors, and other political office holders are the relatives of current and former office holders so that the United States is becoming an inherited monarchy resembling the very British establishment from which the revolutionaries of the 18th century sought to distance themselves by fighting for democracy and against the tyranny of a blood related oligarchy.[23]

V

The League of Women Voters was organized in Chicago on February 14, 1920, six months before the 19th Amendment to the Constitution was ratified. That Amendment gave the vote to American women. This league was the idea of Carrie Chapman Catt, at that time president of the National American Woman Suffrage (Latin suffragium = vote) Association. The first president of the LWV was Maud Wood Park. She did not focus the league exclusively on women's issues, but sought to educate all citizens to participate in the election process.

The early organizers of the league were women who had experience as fighters for voting rights. Some represented the Women's Trade Union League and others the National Consumers League. These women also fought for DC voting rights. Citizens of the District of Columbia can vote for President of the United States according to the 23rd Amendment. However, they cannot vote for Congress because they are not a state.[24]

The League pushed for the establishment of a women's bureau for metropolitan police departments and sought child labor laws which prevented the exploitation of children in factories and coal mines. This led to the Juvenile Delinquency Act of 1938.

The league then lobbied to end the "taxi dance halls," which were invitations to prostitution where young girls were victimized and exploited. Then the league succeeded in having the Civil Service Act extended to DC employees and thereafter supported civil liberties. They opposed the loyalty oaths demanded from government employees in the 1950's and 1960's, and in the 1940's made a study of the DC public schools, leading to higher pay for teachers.

The league favored the work of the United Nations and promoted the Nuclear Non-Proliferation treaty. The League also advocated for public housing for the poor and succeeded in having "age" included in the anti-discrimination laws passed in the 1960's.

In the spirit of gender equality, men were admitted to the League of Women Voters in 1975, a year in which the League also favored legislation concerning gun control.[25]

VI

It has been amply demonstrated that feminist attitudes influence voting patterns in the United States. In fact, political activities of any kind are influenced by feminism, so that feminist women are more likely to support a candidate who agrees to feminist goals than someone who belongs to one party or another.[26]

In the general female population, however, increasing levels of education and income favor greater support for Republican candidates. Furthermore, some specific issues are supported or dismissed on the basis of personal interest. For example, women who work outside the home are more supportive of child care arrangements than those who don't work. Such women are also interested in equal pay for equal work, back family leave, and are unlikely to support military expenditures. Contrary to fact, it is believed by many women that Democrats are more likely to promote these causes than is true of Republicans, so that women who have these interests are likely to vote Democrat because many women believe that the Democrats are more interested in women's rights than is true of Republicans.[27]

The principal tool designed to achieve equality for women is the proposed Equal Rights Amendment. This amendment was first proposed by Alice Paul at the 75th anniversary of the 1848 Women's Rights Convention. The amendment said: "Men and women shall have equal rights throughout the United States and every place subject to its jurisdiction." This amendment was introduced in every session of Congress until it passed in 1972 in slightly altered form. The amendment was then sent to the states with a seven year deadline for ratification. However, only 35 states ratified the amendment, so that it failed to become part of the American Constitution.

Ronald Reagan was the Republican candidate at the presidential election of 1980, and Jimmy Carter, the sitting president, sought a second term as the Democratic candidate. The two candidates differed sharply on women's issues. Reagan opposed the ERA and supported a constitutional amendment to ban abortion but supported legislation that would support "the traditional American family." Carter supported the Equal Rights Amendment, endorsed the Supreme Court decision Roe V. Wade which allowed women to abort, and promoted the notion of equal pay for equal work. Carter also favored the expenditure of federal funds for child care. Reagan won the election. Forty-nine percent of women voted for Reagan, while 53 percent of men voted for Reagan. Feminist women largely voted Democrat, non-feminist women stayed with the Republicans. In subsequent elections, feminists continued to be more supportive of Democrats.[28]

VII

"All politics are local," said Thomas Phillip O'Neil (1910–1994), who was speaker of the House for ten years. It may well be that this phrase was also commonly expressed by others. In any event, it is evident that men and women who seek political office must usually begin their careers in the lower ranking offices of a local nature, such as mayor of a town or city, unless they are extremely wealthy, as is often the case with U.S. Senators or the relatives of office holders.

It is therefore instructive that only 18.4% of the 1,351 mayors of American cities with populations over 30,000 are women. The largest city with a female mayor is Houston, Texas, which has a population of 2,099,451. The smallest community with a female mayor and a population of 30,000 or more is Gallatin, Tennessee. It is not surprising that California, the most populous state, has more female mayors than any other state. New York, with a population of over 18 million, has elected women mayors in only eight communities, of which only Albany has a fairly large population of 98,000.[29]

It is therefore evident that women still hold far fewer elected and appointed political positions than do men. This disparate situation is true of national offices, but also affects local positions such as council members. If we include women who hold offices in small communities of less than 30,000, it is visible that women are just as underrepresented in lower level political positions as in higher offices. It is also evident that the less important an office may be, the greater the possibility that a woman is elected to that office.[30]

The "deficiency hypothesis" holds that female candidates for offices will face more competition from men when tenure is longer and compensation is higher and the prestige of the office is greater.[31]

Research has shown that larger municipalities are more likely to have female representation than is true of small towns and cities. In fact, women occupy more council seats in cities with more affluent or highly educated citizens than is true of those with lesser education and fewer resources. This is in part true because women with more education and resources are more likely recruited to run for an office than is true of less educated and poorer women. Better educated women are more likely to have the time and the talent needed to run for an office and to carry out its responsibilities once elected.[32]

A recent study has shown that there are regional variations in the participation of women in the electoral process. The South and Northeast are less hospitable to women seeking office than is true of other regions of the country.[33]

Also, larger municipalities are more likely to have chapters of the League of Women Voters, the National Organization for Women, and other groups determined to help women gain election. In larger communities there are more women's rights groups active in promoting women's agendas, including election to political office. The best example of such an organization is the National Women's Political Caucus. This organization actively works for the election of women and constitutes an intermediary between a female candidate and the electorate.[34]

The most common route to elected office for women is election to council member and from there to mayor. The Mayoral Recruitment Study has shown that the vast majority of female mayors had begun their career as council members or in other minor positions. The success of some women in gaining these offices leads others to consider running for offices and paves the way for those who succeed in becoming members of state legislatures and members of Congress.[35]

Women candidates for elected office have to contend with an issue seldom applied to men. Evidently, voters judge women candidates largely on their appearance. This has been well documented by a study carried out at Dartmouth College by Jonathan Freeman and other psychologists. These researchers examined "how the typicality of gender cues in politicians' faces related to electoral success." The major finding was that some voters decide within a millisecond after viewing a politician's face whether or not to vote for her. This decision is more frequent among conservative voters, who are more likely to expect a feminine appearance of the candidate than is true of most "liberal" voters. However, the study also found that a female candidate with a masculine face has hardly any chance of election by the majority of American voters.[36]

Women politicians face yet another obstacle. That is the "double bind" of being assertive, self-reliant, and independent, as well as nurturing and likeable but incompetent. Women who demonstrate the assertiveness expected of men are viewed as unfeminine. This leads the candidate's publicity projects to display her as charming and approachable or competent but masculine. The 2008 campaign for president reflected this when Sarah Palin, former governor of Alaska and Republican candidate for Vice President, was portrayed by the media as likable, feminine, but incompetent, while Hillary Clinton was depicted as ambitious, forceful, competent, and not very likeable. In fact, some of the posters and other advertisements against the Clinton candidacy were embarrassing and gross in language and illustrations.

One TV commentator said that "men won't vote for Hillary Clinton because she reminds them of their nagging wives," while another commented that Clinton was supported by those who felt sorry for her because her husband, President Bill Clinton, is an adulterer.[37]

The consequences of these portrayals are also visible in the world of business and industry. Although women are half the non-farm work force, they hold only about 16% of corporate Fortune 500 board seats and 3% of Fortune 500 CEO positions. Moreover, women earn only 89% of what men earn in business and other occupations.[38]

Women seeking political office have to contend with yet other stereotypes. It is commonly believed that women are less task oriented than men. This means that public perception holds that women are more likely than men to leave a task in order to help someone in need or to tend to children or to promote community needs. This should be seen as a positive trait but is viewed by many voters as an obstacle in working consistently at the political job.[39]

It is significant that region of the country is associated with the election of women. Evidently, the southern culture is less likely to permit women to gain political office than is true in other parts of the country. This means that traditionally the South put women on a pedestal which required women to be inactive, unaggressive, and willing to be dominated by men. This view is of course less common at the beginning of the 21st century than in earlier years because the South has been greatly altered since 1970, as more and more northerners have moved there and brought with them beliefs and attitudes not usually held by traditional southern culture.[40]

Those who hold a political office, so-called incumbents (incumbare is Latin "to lean down") have a number of advantages over those seeking an office. They have name recognition, access to major donors, and a staff who have previous experience in getting their candidate elected. A woman, new to politics, has no such advantages and is therefore less likely to defeat an incumbent man.[41]

Politicians have the reputation of being selfish, power hungry, and greedy. Yet, a study by Abrahams concludes that women politicians are motivated for political activity by a chance to benefit the community rather than for personal gain. That study also concluded that women see themselves as giving rather than receiving benefits through political activities.[42]

In view of the obstacles that traditionally faced women interested in a political career, it is not surprising that the number of girls interested in politics is a good deal less than is true of boys. Therefore, women who have attained public office should become a role model for girls, in that winning female politicians are in effect telling girls that they can look forward to entering politics if they chose.

This means that the presence of female politicians legitimizes the efforts of women to run for office and increases the interest women and girls have in politics and in the possibility that they will try to gain election themselves.[43]

The most effective means of interesting girls in politics is discussion with parents concerning political actions such as voting, campaigning for a candidate by distributing literature or making phone calls and/or contributing money. This may well be the most effective means of creating women candidates for office but is underutilized. The evidence for this is that women are responsible for 2 million fewer phone calls than is true of men. No doubt boys are more often introduced to politics by their parents than is true of girls.[44]

VIII

The future of American women in politics will therefore be determined in part by the willingness of younger women to enter into the political arena. That willingness in turn will be determined by the possibility of success in getting women elected to political offices. There can be no doubt that women have indeed progressed a good deal over the last several decades in attaining political power. That is in part due to organizations devoted to bringing about female success in the political arena.

One of these organizations is the National Women's Political Caucus. This group was founded in 1971 as an answer to Congress failing to pass the Civil Rights Amendment. This organization was conceived by Congresswoman Bella Abzug and also endorsed by Gloria Steinem, Betty Friedan, and a number of other visible activists in the women's rights movement. These women believed that economic and social equality for women could only be achieved when women were equally represented among the nation's political decision makers.[45]

The first success the NWPC recorded was the threefold increase in delegates to the Democratic National Conventions between 1968 and 1972. That increase was achieved because the NWPC was well represented on the McGovern Commission, which had been formed to consider the increase in female delegates to these conventions. Subsequently the NWPC created a Democratic and a Republican Task Force. The NWPC also influenced the Supreme Court decision in Roe V. Wade, which found the right of women to favor an abortion to be constitutional and legal.[46]

The NWPC organizes campaign workshops across the country, which teach would-be candidates how to run a successful campaign. They also consider candidates for endorsement who are supported by financial action committees. They also teach politicians how to gain political appointments and collaborate with other women's groups in endorsing women who seek appointed offices.

Notes

1. Robert Sobel, Biographical Directory of the Governors of the United States, vol.4, (Westport,CT: Meckler Books 1978).

2. Shelley Salee, "The Woman of It: Governor Miriam Ferguson's 1924 Election," Southwestren Historical Quarterly, vol. 100, (July 1996):1–16.

3. 19th Amendment to the Constitution of the United States.

4. Lynn Sweet, "Pritzker appointed Secretary of Commerce," Chicago Sun-Times, (May 2, 2013):1.

5. Center for American Women and Politics, (New Brusnswick: Rutgers, The State University of New Jersey). Fact Sheet, No date.

6. Jennifer Liberto, "New peek into Caroline Kennedy's Wealth," Money, (August 19, 2013):1.

7. Susan M. Schafer, "S.C. Gov. Haley's Husband Deploys with Guard, Army Times, (January 10, 2013):1.

8. Daniel Greenfield, "Front Page Magazine," (August 28, 2012):1.

9. Robert Slater and Elaine Slater. Great Jewish Women, (Middle Village, NY: Jonathan David. Publisher, 2004):78.

10. Biographlcal Directory of the United States Congress, (C.Q. Staff Directories, 2004).

11. Dianne Feinstein, Biographical Directory of the United States Congress.

12. Sean Laughlin and Robert Yoon, "Millionaires Populate U.S. Senate," All Politics, (June 13, 2003).

13. Hillary Rodham Clinton, Living History, (New York: Simon and Schuster, 2003) and Hard Choices, (New York: Simon and Schuster, 2014).

14. Debra Fischer, Biographical Directory of the U.S. Congress, (Washington DC: The United States Government Printing Office, 2013).

15. Jay Newton-Small and Zeke J. Miller, "Talent at the Top," Time, vol. 184, no. 20 (November 24, 2014).

16. "Kay Bailey Hutchinson," Biographical Directory of the United States Congress. (Washington DC: U.S. Government Printing Office, 2005).

17. "Lisa Murkowski," (Washington, DC, Biographical Directory of the United States Congress, 2010).

18. http://www.politico.com/magazine/story/2015/01/senate-women-secret-history-113908_Page2.html#.VWSK-tHbKEU [accessed May 26, 2015].

19. Hilary Burns, "There are 100 women in Congress for the first time in history," Business First, (November 5, 2014):1.

20. Freedom House, Freedom in the World, 2013.

21. U.S. Department of Commerce, Bureau of the Census, (Washington, DC: United States Government Printing Office, 2013.)

22. Laurel Elder, "Contrasting Party Dynamics" Social Science Journal, vol.51, No.3, (September 2014):377–385.

23. G.C. Jacobson, Politics of Congressional Elections, (New York: Pearson, 2012).

24. Constitution of the United States, Amendment XXIII.

25. League of Women Voters.History of the League of Women Voters (Washington DC, 2011).

26. Clyde Wilcox, "The causes and consequences of feminist consciousness," Comparative Political Studies, vol. 23, (1991):519–545.

27. Elizabeth Cook and Clyde Wilcox, "Feminism and the Gender Gap," Journal of Politics, vol.53, (1991):1111–1122.

28. Kristan McMurran, "Reagan is Shortchanging Women, Says GOP Feminist Kathy Wilson," People, vol. 20, no. 5, (August 1, 1983):1.

29. Center for American Women and Politics, "Women Mayors in U.S. Cities 2014," (New Brunswick, NJ: Eagelton Institute of Politics, 2014).

30. Susan Welch and Albert K. Karnig, "Correlates of female office holding in city politics," Journal of Politics, vol. 41, (1979):478–491.

31. David B. Hill, "Political Culture and Female Political Representation," Journal of Politics, vol. 43, (1981):159–168.

32. Kira Sanbonmatsu, Susan B. Carroll, and Debbi Walsh, "Poised to Run: Women's Pathway to the State Legislatures," (New Brunswick, NJ: Rutgers: The State University of New Jersey, 2009).

33. Trounstine and Valdine:69.

34. Ann Marshall, "Organizing Across the Divide," Social Science Quarterly, vol.83 (2002):707–725.

35. Susan J. Carroll and Kira Sanbonmatsu, "Entering the Mayor's Office: Women's Decisions to Run for Municipal Office," (Chicago: The Midwest Political Science Association, 2010).

36. Jonathan Freeman, Eric Heiman, Collen M. Carpinella, Kerri L. Johnson, Jordan B. Leitner, "Early Processing of Gender Cues Predicts the Electoral Success of Female Politicians," Social Psychological and Personality Science. Vol. 5, no.7 (September 2014):815–824.

37. "Your World with Neil Cavuto," FOX News TV Broadcast. January 4, 2008.

38. Sam Roberts, "For Young Earners in Big City, Gap Shifts in Women's Favor," (New York Times, August 3, 2007):A1.

39. Madeline E. Heilman, "Description and Prescription: How Gender Stereotypes Prevent Women's Ascent up the Organizational Ladder," Journal of Social Issues, vol. 57, (2001):658.

40. T. Rice and D.L. Coates, "Gender Role Attitudes in the Southern United States," Gender and Society, vol. 9, no.6, (1995):744.

41. Bruce Palmer and David Simon, "The Political Glass Ceiling: Gender, Strategy and Incumbency," Women and Politics, vol. 23, no2, (2001):259.

42. N. Abrahams, ""Negotiating Power, Identity, Family and Community," Gender and Society, vol.10, no.6, (1996):768.

43. Nancy Burns, Kay L. Schlossman and Sidney Verba, The Private Roots of Gender Action, (Cambridge: Harvard University Press, 2001).

44. Michael X. Delli Carpini and Scott Keeter, What Americans Know About Politics, (New Haven: Yale University Press, 1996).

45. http://www.nwpc.org./history [accessed July 9, 2015].

46. Ginette Castro, American Feminism. (Paris, France: National Political Science Press):200.

Chapter Five

Women in the Military

I

Anyone who joins the American military will inevitably face a severe "culture shock." This means that all those assumptions an American citizen expects to encounter every day are absent from the military. This refers to the rights and freedoms which American citizens expect because they are enshrined in the constitution and assumed to exist without further question.

The military treat enlisted women and men in a manner not far from the treatment endured by federal prisoners. Like prisoners, military personnel cannot quit their job at will. If enlisted for three years, the women and men in the military have to stay there as long as the enlistment continues. Soldiers also face a hierarchy so segmented and rigid that the new recruit enters a world reminiscent of Prussia in the nineteenth century. Soldiers are expected to salute every time they happen to walk past an officer. Unlike the dictum that "all men are created equal," the military teach that all men and women are unequal. And that the lowest ranking soldiers, called "privates," have about the same standing as erstwhile plantation slaves.

The military is close to being a large prison. The normal constitutional guarantees included in the first ten amendments do not apply to the military, which has its own code of military justice, a most brutal means of suppressing all initiative or possible dissent.

An example of this king of suppression is reported by Gutmann. She observed how some young male recruits ran competition although told by their drill sergeant to run in a circle until he returned. This "initiative" was immediately stopped by a female drill sergeant, who could not tolerate even this mild expression of initiative.[1]

Freedom of speech and freedom of the press do not exist in the U.S. armed forces. Instead, all soldiers must conform to the opinion of their "superiors." These "superiors" are all non-commissioned and commissioned officers who have absolute power over those whose rank is beneath them.

How can those deprived of all freedom and rights be expected to fight and possibly die for a freedom they do not possess? This antiquated means of conducting our defenses dates from the days of 18th century Prussian methods introduced by Count von Steuben during the Revolutionary War but not efficient today. Women recruits into the armed forces are faced with these conditions.

There are slightly more than 214,000 female service women in the U.S. armed forces. These women account for no more than 15% of the armed forces of the United States. Because they are such a small minority, women have the advantage of being highly desirable amidst so many sex starved men. Yet, the same one sided sex ratio also includes the hazard of sexual assault, which has been the source of a major complaint on the part of female soldiers.[2]

Sexual assault is common in the armed forces. According to a most recent report, an estimated 26,000 instances of sexual assault took place in the military in one year, despite the publicity given these crimes and despite the condemnation of such conduct by President Obama.[3]

It is significant that two officers charged with preventing sexual assault were themselves accused of "fondling women" and "groping women in a parking lot." The first accusation was directed at Air Force Lt. Colonel Jeff Kusinski, who was arrested and charged with sexual battery in May of 2013. This led the then Secretary of Defense, Chuck Hagel, to express outrage and disgust at these allegations.[4]

On May 15, 2013 the media reported that the Army Sexual Assault Prevention Office Coordinator was accused of abusive sexual contact and that Lt. Colonel James Wilkerson was found guilty of "abusive sexual conduct and aggravated sexual assault." That conviction was reversed by Air Force Lt. General Craig Franklin.[5]

Brigadier General Jeffrey A. Sinclair, stationed at Fort Bragg, NC, pleaded not guilty to eight criminal charges, including forcible sodomy, indecent acts, violating order,s and conduct unbecoming an officer. Sinclair admitted to a three year extramarital relationship with a junior female officer. Since adultery is a crime under military law, this admission alone ended his 28 year career in the army.[6]

These examples of sexual misconduct in the armed services demonstrate that the puritan approach to sex practiced there cannot work and is misguided. Indeed, tradition demands that 17h century Puritanism be the guide to 21st century behavior. Yet, nature and the evolution of American society denies this effort to suppress sexual interest in a country in which 41 percent of children are born to single mothers and condoms are distributed to high school students.

Nevertheless, there is a good deal of criticism of the armed forces because of the publicity given to sexual harassment and assault. The critics argue that the armed forces constitute a more disciplined segment of society than civilian life, that the military should be held to a "higher standard" than civilians, and that military law is responsible for failure to eliminate sexual assault. Yet, the personnel of the armed forces derive from the civilian population and are not created in a vacuum.[7]

The truth is that sexual assault also occurs in civilian life and is particularly induced by alcohol consumption both in the military and in civilian life. The Department of Justice found in 2011 that sexual assault occurs in only 0.9 victims per thousand people in the population. However, the Centers for Disease Control found that in a 12 month period, 5.6% of women suffered sexual violence and 1.1 percent were raped.[8] It has also been noted that college students, who are within the same age cohort as newly enlisted soldiers, are sexually assaulted at the same ratio as is true in the military.[9]

As is true in civilian life, victims of sexual assault are reluctant to report this to authorities not only because many fear having to recite the details in court, but also because they have experienced that the judiciary does not do anything for them. In fact, it is well known that victims of rape and other sex offenses are often subjected to embarrassment and insult. Women in the military face yet another obstacle which is determined by nature. This refers to muscular endurance, strength, power, aerobic capacity and performance of specific tasks. In all of these areas women are less capable than men, although in combat situations they may face conditions requiring male capacity.[10]

The ability to lift and carry has always been an important attribute to success in combat. Now that the Department of Defense has allowed women to be combat soldiers, the issue of muscular strength has become important. Thus, "fighting loads" are reported at 29 kg, which is equal to 64 lbs. So called "approach loads" weigh about 101 lbs. and "emergency approach" loads average 60 kilograms or 132 lbs. These heavy loads are responsible for numerous injuries among men and are almost impossible for most women.[11]

There are those who contend that women should not be allowed in infantry units because the presence of women lessens the fighting effectiveness of any infantry unit. This argument is based in part on the view that infantry soldiers are young men who should be concentrating on the business of being a fighter, not distracted by women. It is claimed that the lifting of the ban on women in combat was based on "political correctness" and not on the facts of military needs.

Another argument against the participation of women in combat is that so many women get pregnant in the service and therefore need to be discharged. The rate of single motherhood in the military is 14 percent. A unit which loses the service of a female member becomes less effective even If a replacement can be found to take the place of the vacancy caused by pregnancy.[12]

There were also those who claimed that the inclusion of women into the armed forces would lead to its "feminization," with the consequence that this would diminish the fighting ability of the services.[13] Yet, a number of female soldiers have proved this view as wrong, as illustrated by Sergeant Leigh Ann Hester, who won the Army's Silver Star because of her initiative in successfully fighting off insurgents in Iraq who had attacked an American convoy. There were numerous other such actions by military women deployed in Iraq and Afghanistan.[14]

In addition some Americans view all military personnel as "trained killers." They see the military as a brutal occupation to be disdained by "decent" people.[15]

All of these arguments against the inclusion of women in the armed forces became spurious when the draft was ended in 1973. This led to the concern that the armed forces would not be able to attract enough men into the all volunteer force. The concern was unfounded, as the participation of women climbed from 2% in 1973 to 12% in 1993 and 15% in 2003, where it has remained.[16]

As a result, women were involved in Operation Desert Shield in 1990 and in Desert Storm in 1991. About 40,000 women participated in the first Persian Gulf war, which represented about 7% of the U.S. forces. At that time women were allowed to fly refueling planes but were not allowed to fly combat aircraft, although they were just as vulnerable in the refueling planes as anyone in a combat plane.

The absurdity of these rules was fueled by a contempt for women among naval and Marine aviators, as demonstrated by the "Tail Hook Convention" held in Las Vegas in 1991. There, 26 women were groped and molested as they passed through a gauntlet of male aviators. High ranking officers did nothing to stop the debauchery. In 1996, male drill sergeants were found to assault women soldiers at the Aberdeen Proving Grounds. Both incidents revealed disrespect tor women service personnel, preventing women from pursuing careers in the military.[17]

Sexual harassment and discrimination also exist in civilian life. Therefore it is instructive that the General Social Survey conducted by the National Opinion Research Center at the University of Chicago found that white women soldiers are slightly more satisfied with their jobs than white civilian women and that black women soldiers are twice as likely to be satisfied with their military jobs than black civilian women.[18]

For centuries, warfare has been associated with manliness. This has become so ingrained in almost all cultures that it seems incongruous to attribute this feature to women as well.

II

In the second decade of the 21st century, the presence of women in the armed forces of the United States is nothing new. In fact, women have had minor roles in every war this country has ever fought. Molly Pitcher actually assumed her wounded husband's duties as a cannoneer during the American Revolution, as did Deborah Samson, who disguised herself as a man so that she could participate in the Revolution. Likewise, Lucy Brewer did the same thing during the War of 1812.During the Civil War, women served as nurses and spies, and in World War I, 20,000 women served in the army and navy as nurses. In addition, 12,500 women served in the U.S. Naval Reserve and 300 women served in the U.S. Marines as camouflage designers, recruiters, and clerks.[19]

The most important contribution of women to the war effort in all the wars of the United States was made by nurses.

When nurses first joined the U.S. military during the First World War in 1917, they were given no rank, leaving these women without support of any kind and at the discretion of male officers. This led to a major effort on the part of women within and outside the military to give nurses officer's standing so as to avoid the hostile environment to which they were subject.[20]

The effort to give military nurses an officer's rank coincided with the suffrage movement, which sought to give women the right to vote in federal elections. Therefore the National Women's Suffrage Association adopted a resolution asking Congress to give military ranks to army nurses.[21]

The struggle to gain a military rank for military nurses continued for thirty-seven years, until Congress finally passed the Army-Navy Nurses Act of 1947 and the Women's Armed Services Integration Act of 1948. With this legislation, women received commission, pay, and benefits commensurate with their rank.[22]

As the weapons of war became more and more deadly, leading also to an increase in the number of the wounded, nurses reduced the number of deaths and permanent disabilities by their skill and dedication. As soon as the Japanese had attacked the United States on December 7, 1941, organized nurses supported the war effort. This was possible because at the American Nurses Association convention in 1938, the Army Nurse Corps announced that it had increased its strength from 600 to 675. This led to the formation of the National Nursing Council for War in 1940.[23]

During the Second World War, 100,000 out of 173,000 employed nurses had volunteered, and 76,000 had actually served in the army or navy nurse corps.[24]

During the war, a Cadet Nurse Corps was established by the American Nurses Association. This was an effort to increase the number of nurses available not only in wartime but also in peacetime. The corps allocated funds to 1125 schools, which enrolled 170,000 students.[25]

During the Second World War the Women's Army Corps was established by Congress and Women Accepted for Voluntary Emergency Services (WaVES) were accepted by the Navy. The marines and coast guard established similar units.[26]

A major effort by all units of the U.S. military community to recruit more women failed during the Second World War because men generally resented the presence of women in jobs behind the front, which had protected men from the dangers of combat until a woman took the place of a man thereupon sent to fight. Men claimed thatwas fou military women were promiscuous or lesbians, a rumor widely distributed by the media. This led to a major decline in the number of women willing to serve.[27]

As the Second World War progressed, the need for fighting men became acute, as the U.S. fought a two front war in Asia and in Europe. Indeed, eleven million men were in uniform in 1943. Of these men, 1.3 million were doing jobs which could be done by women. Yet these jobs were never filled entirely by women because of the slander campaign and because most, but not all, men were adamantly opposed to the female military. While the other services would not let women go overseas, the army and air force succeeded in landing 4,715 women soldiers in England in 1944, where they were assigned work as photographers, interpreters, censors, and cryptographers.

The involvement of women in the army and navy during the Second World War led to a more permanent and even career oriented participation of women thereafter. This became evident when the Women's Army Auxiliary Corps was changed to the Women's Army Corps, leading to requests by field commanders to increase the number of women recruited.[28]

The U.S. Air Force, at first called the U.S. Army Air Force, was more successful than the other branches of the defense establishment in recruiting women. In 1942, during World War II, when a severe shortage of male pilots developed, the Air Force turned to women to fill the gap. A Women Air Force Service Pilots or WASPS group was trained to fly military aircraft so that men could be relieved and fly combat missions instead of dealing with non-combat issues. As a result, more than 1,100 women flew almost every type of military aircraft, including even the heavy bombers labeled B26 and B29 bombers. They ferried new planes long distances from factories to military bases and towed targets so that Air Force pilots could practice shooting with live ammunition. Despite these successes, the program was cancelled after two years.[29]

Among those who volunteered to fly for the Army Air Force in those days was Margaret Phelan Taylor. She was nineteen and had just finished two years of college. She earned a pilot's license and then flew to Avenger Field in Sweetwater, Texas, to join the WASPs.

Mabel Rawlinson was another female volunteer pilot in World War II. She was killed in a plane crash at Camp Davis, NC during a training exercise. Although she died in the service of her country, the military did not pay for her funeral because she was a civilian.

The WASP program was ended in 1944 and it appeared that there would never be women in the U.S. Air Force. Yet in 1976 the Air Force announced that women would be allowed to fly. The original WASPS had been forgotten until they lobbied Congress to be militarized, which they achieved with the help of then Senator Barry Goldwater of Arizona.[30]

Years later, in 1993, women first received fighter pilot training, so that by 2015, 18.9% of the 13,216 pilots in the Air Force are women. Nineteen percent of officers and 18% of enlisted corps are women. More than half, I.e. 55%, of women officers are line officers, which is true of 48% of men. There are 58,560 women in the Air Force of 309,339 active duty members.[31]

III

After lengthy debate in the media and in Congress, the House and Senate passed the Women's Armed Services Integration Act in 1948.[32] It then took another twenty-eight years before women were admitted to the service academies, including the U.S. Military Academy at West Point, NY, The Naval Academy at Annapolis, MD, and the Air Force Academy at Colorado Springs, CO. In 1980, 62 female cadets graduated West Point. Since then more than 4,000 women have graduated and more have applied, as the Department of Defense has opened combat positions to women beginning in 2016. This may well mean that up to 20% of the class of 2019 will be women.[33]

An inspection of the curriculum of the service academies provides us with a view of three difficult and demanding academic loads for those fortunate enough to be so employed. At West Point, the Army Military Academy lists eighteen majors, including chemical, civil, mechanical, nuclear, and environmental engineering. Also included are non-mathematical studies, such as American Politics, Art, Philosophy and Literature, Foreign Areas Studies, Foreign Languages and Legal Studies. In addition, the curriculum includes Mathematical Science, Life Science,, Legal Studies and Environmental Geography.

Similar education is available at the U.S. Naval Academy. There too the physical sciences dominate, although Arabic and Chinese as well as English may be selected as majors. The Naval Academy also provides for a major in History and Economics. The academy's motto is: "We Build Intellectuals, Leaders, and Success Stories."

The Air Force Academy program includes 27 majors. These include Aeronautical Engineering, Civil Engineering, Electrical Engineering, Geopolitical Science, Foreign Area Studies, History, and others. There is also a Merchant Marine Academy and a Coast Guard Academy.

These academies charge no tuition. Applicants must be nominated by a member of Congress.[34]

Women did not easily gain access to the service academies. In fact, it took a number of years and several lawsuits to make the entrance of women into the academies a reality. The arguments against women becoming military officers were based in part on tradition. Another argument was that women were excluded from participating in combat. Since the academies taught cadets how to deal with combat situations, it seemed useless and wasteful to accept women who could never use what they had learned. Prohibition against women in combat extended to the role of women as air force pilots.[35]

Even Jacqueline Cochran, the leader of the Women's Air Service Pilots in World War II, testified against the entrance of women into the military academies. Yet, after lengthy debate, Congress finally passed a bill opening the service academies to women on June 30, 1975, effective in 1976. The law prohibited separate training for women cadets.[36]

The Air Force Academy proceeded to integrate women into the Corps of Cadets by appointing the sociologist Lois De Fleur to the Department of Behavioral Sciences, where she served for one year, leading to an establishment of a curriculum for both men and women and promoting the recruiting of women athletes into the academies.[37]

As more and more women graduated, a debate concerning women in combat ensued in Congress and in the media, although women had already participated in combat during the 1990 Panama invasion and in Operation Desert Storm in 1990–1991, when 15 women were killed and others wounded or taken prisoner.[38]

It became inevitable that women who had graduated from the U.S. military academies would become generals and admirals. These high ranks in the armed services are attained by understanding the politics of the defense industry. For example, General Dwight Eisenhower, later to become the 34th President of the United States, never experienced a shot fired in earnest. Instead he commanded others, who were killed, wounded, and imprisoned. Eisenhower took all the credit for the sacrifices made by others. Likewise, these tactics served other generals over the years and are equally available to women.

Janet Wolfenbarger is a four star general. She was promoted to that rank in 2009. A graduate of an engineering college, she heads the Air Force Material Command at the Dayton, Ohio air force base. That is a position equal to civilian executive assignments such as the presidency of General Motors, now held by Mary Barra. There can be no doubt that women can oversee such an installation as well as any man.[39]

Until her retirement from the Army, General Ann Dunwoody was commander of the Army Material Command in Huntsville, Alabama. She was promoted to a four star general in 2011. She moved into a home in Redstone Arsenal at that time with her husband, retired Air Force Colonel Craig Brotchie. The Army Material Command deals with the development of sophisticated weapons systems and research as well as maintenance and distribution of spare parts. The command includes 69,000 soldiers and civilians. Dunwoody served in the army for thirty-seven years.[40]

The U.S. Navy has been even more accommodating to women than the Army. Eleven women hold the rank of rear admiral, four women are vice admirals and one woman, Michelle Howard, is an admiral. Howard was appointed vice chief of naval operations in July of 2014. She commanded Task Force 151, which dealt with counter piracy operations in the Gulf of Aden in 2009.[41]

Captain Kathleen McGrath was the first woman to command an American Navy warship. In the spring of 2000 she became commander of the frigate Jarrett a 453 foot warship with a 262 member crew. She sailed into the northernmost reaches of the Persian Gulf to prevent the smuggling of Iranian oil. She had graduated from the University of California at Sacramento. In 1980 she decided to follow her father into the Air Force but was persuaded to join the Navy instead. Before being deployed to the Persian Gulf, she also served in the Western Pacific, the Mediterranean and the Caribbean Sea. In 1993 and 1994 she commanded the salvage ship Recovery and was then appointed to The Joint Advanced Warfighting Unit. She was honored with the Legion of Merit and the Meritorious Service Medals.[42]

Another former commander of an American naval ship is Holly Graf. She was captain of the guided missile cruiser USS Cowpens, stationed in Japan. In 2010 she was dismissed as commander of that 400 crew ship because she abused the crew in a most offensive manner. Graf evidently swore at other officers and enlisted sailors, used foul language, and rejected all efforts to placate her unreasonable outbursts of anger. A report by the Inspector General concluded that she was not fit to command a naval ship, leading to her early retirement from the Navy.[43]

IV

The burden of defending the country lies almost entirely on the shoulders of those who risk life and limb in combat against our enemies. The vast majority of those who died or were wounded in combat are men, because men constitute 85% percent of the armed forces of the United States. The 15% female service members have shown that they were and are as ready to die for their country as men have always demonstrated.

It was the decision to allow women in combat that led to the wounding and death of women engaged in the fighting in Iraq and Afghanistan. Prior to that decision, the Department of Defense was guided by the Risk Rule, which excluded women from any position which had a high risk, preventing women from engaging in ground combat, hostile fire, or capture.[44]

In 2013 the Secretary of Defense, Leon Panetta, and General Martin Dempsey, Chairman of the Joint Chiefs of Staff, lifted the Department of Defense ban on women in combat. That new rule overturned the 1994 rule that restricted women from artillery, armor, infantry and other combat roles. In fact, a number of women had already participated in the war in Iraq and Afghanistan, so that 800 women had been wounded and more than 130 had died at the time the policy was changed. The move to allow women in combat was provoked by a letter written by General Dempsey, who recommended the inclusion of women in combat.[45]

In part, this change was prompted by a lawsuit filed by the American Civil Liberties Union which sought to support Major Mary Jennings Hagar, a helicopter pilot. Hagar was wounded when her plane was shot down but could not seek any leadership positions because the defense department would not acknowledge the experience of women in combat. Because career advancement in all the services depends on combat experience, women who fought for the country prior to the changing of the rules could not advance in the military hierarchy.[46]

Since the lives of both men and women were already at risk in both Iraq and Afghanistan, it became evident that women had to be acknowledged as front line fighters.

It is also significant that a 2013 public opinion poll conducted by the Pew Research Center showed that a majority of the participants believed that combat roles for women would not harm military effectiveness. Two thirds of the participants supported allowing women in the military to serve in ground units that engage in close combat. Only 26% opposed this.

Another poll conducted in January of 2004 among 1,005 adults resulted in an almost even split among the participants as to whether combat roles represent a major change in policies concerning military women. Moreover, 58% of those polled believed that these policy changes will improve career opportunities for military women. Nearly one half of respondents thought that military effectiveness would not be changed in either direction because of the participation of women.

In short, it is evident that the participation of women in all aspects of military life is a permanent aspect of women's rise to ascendancy in American life.[47]

This acknowledgement was a radical change from centuries old traditions, as for most of history women were excluded from combat roles. In fact, women were employed in the armed services of all countries as nurses and sometimes in clerical positions, but not as combatants. Then, in the 1970's, American women were gradually permitted to serve in such support roles as military police, maintenance, engineering, and signaling. Infantry and armored units excluded women because these positions involved direct contact with the enemy.

This gradual integration of women into the armed forces began when in 1967 the United States abolished the quota system which limited women to 2% of enlisted personnel and 10% of officers. In the 1990's, legal restrictions on the roles of women in the armed forces were also removed, although the Direct Ground Combat Definition and Assignment Rule was imposed. This rule held that: "Women shall be excluded from assignment in units below the brigade level whose primary mission is to engage in direct combat on the ground ... etc."[48]

This rule excluded women from infantry, armor, artillery, combat engineering, air defense artillery, and special forces. This rule was based on the assumption that wars would continue to be fought from forward positions and rear support areas. That assumption has proved wrong in the Iraq and Afghanistan wars, where anyone may have been an enemy disguised as a civilian and where roadside bombs and all kinds of booby traps killed and wounded soldiers anywhere. This led the U.S. military to use women soldiers on patrol in order to search Muslim women.[49]

In fact, there was no "front" in these wars. The U.S. forces traveled in convoys, which experienced a threat from all sides at any time and were subject to rockets and ambushes. As a result, 152 service women were killed between 9/11/2001 and January 2013.[50]

Finally, one hundred and sixty military women were killed in the "War on Terror" in Iraq and Afghanistan. They were not the first to die in battle. In 1775,

Jemima Warner was killed by an enemy bullet during the siege of Quebec. Warner was an American who accompanied her husband fighting for the British against the French.

The first American women to die in the First World War were Army nurses Edith Ayres and Helen Wood. Both nurses were on board a ship, the USS Mongolia, when the crew fired the deck guns, killing both nurses.

In World War II 543 women died "in the line of duty." Sixteen were killed by enemy fire, the others were killed by accidents or by illness. Seventeen military nurses died during the Korean War and eight women died while serving in the Vietnam War. Sixteen women died during operation Desert Storm. The greatest loss of life among American military women has occurred between September 11, 2001 and the end of 2014, when American forces were largely withdrawn from Iraq and Afghanistan.

Among the one hundred and sixty women killed in Iraq and Afghanistan was Elizabeth Jacobson, who died on September 28, 2005 when an explosive device hit her vehicle in Iraq. She was the first female "Airman" killed in the line of duty. She had been in Iraq just over three months. She was awarded the Award for Expeditionary Excellence, which has been named after her since then. Her citation read: "A1C Jacobson was a great troop... always sought the hardest challenges and never gave up. She worked very hard to get on the convoy section and had only been working it for a couple of weeks when the incident occurred. She was a bright and intelligent young lady who cared deeply for her country and the military." The main gate at Goodfellow Air Force Base in Texas was named after her.

Another female soldier killed in Afghanistan was First Lt. Roslyn Schulte, who died at age 25 from wounds suffered in a roadside bomb attack. She was the first female graduate of the US Air Force Academy to be killed in action. She was awarded the Intelligence Medal for Valor.[51]

Lt. Schulte was traveling from camp Eggers in Kabul to Bagram Airfield to participate in a Joint Task Force Intelligence Sharing Conference.

He funeral was at Temple Israel in St. Louis.

Sgt. Erica Aleicksen was killed by a roadside bomb in Afghanistan on July 8, 2012. She was a native of Putnam County in central Georgia. She joined the army directly after graduating from high school and served in the 978th Military Police Brigade.

The oldest American woman killed in Afghanistan was Meredith L. Howard. She was 52 at the time of her death, resulting from the explosion of a device detonated near a Humvee in which she was behind the gun. She built a wooden box to stand on so she could see over the turret. She was 34 years old when she joined the army reserves. She was deployed because of a shortage of women soldiers. Howard had been a firefighter in Texas, where she was born. She married a manufacturer of fireworks shortly before going to Afghanistan.[52]

Marine Staff Sergeant Lori Anne Privette was killed when her Huey heli-copter crashed at Camp Pendleton, CA. during a training flight on January 23, 2004. She was 27 years old. She had joined the Marines in 1994 and served in Iraq in Operation Freedom. She survived the fighting in Iraq only to be killed in an accident at home.

Sharon T. Swartworth was 43 years old when she died as her helicopter was shot down in Iraq on November 7, 2003. She was the regimental warrant officer for the Judge Advocates General Office. She was the mother of an eight year old son at the time of her death. She was married to a naval captain. She had been in the service for 26 years and hoped to retire soon.

Lauren Blasir Salton Clark M.D. died on February 1, 2003 when space shut-tle Columbia and the entire crew were killed during entry, just 16 minutes before landing. She is survived by her husband and their child. In 1987 she earned a doctorate in medicine and then specialized in pediatrics. The next year she joined the navy and participated in submarine diving exercises. Later she be-came a Naval flight surgeon and subsequently volunteered for training with NASA in space flights.

Anissa Ann Shero was born October 5, 1970 and died in a military plane in Afghanistan on June 13, 2002 at age 31. She was married to Nathan Shero, a special forces airman. She enlisted in 1992 and became the first Air Force wom-an to die in Afghanistan. She was the daughter of Clyde Shuttleworth, a Vi-etnam veteran. She is buried at Arlington national cemetery.

V

Military women are confronted with a decision which affects them more than men. That decision was whether to stay in the military if they have children. Indeed the length of time a military woman or man remains in the service is af-fected by the length of time already served. No doubt those who have been en-rolled for a number of years are more likely to remain and collect the benefits of long service later. Nevertheless, women who are pregnant or have children need to consider their offspring as well. Mothers have to deal with a considerable emotional strain if separated from their children for a long time so that it be-comes a major problem to place one's career ahead of spending time with chil-dren.[53]

After the attack on the World Trade Center in 2001, Private Christina Carde, the mother of a young son, decided to deploy in Afghanistan, thereby leaving her child. She was criticized for this by R. Cort Kirkwood, a "conserva-tive" journalist who was in turn criticized for failing to understand the close re-lationship of soldiers to one another, which his critics viewed as more important than mother-child connections. From the military view, cohesion among soldiers is viewed as the most important relationship in the lives of the military.[54]

Another difficulty mothers as well as fathers face after a long absence from their families is reintegration. This means missing important "milestones" in the life of a child, such as birthdays, graduations, and religious events. Absent parents also lose authority in the family and lose parent-child attachment.[55]

Absentee parents also create separation anxiety in children. This has been described as a state of worry, sadness, and guilt in the sense that children will believe that it is their fault that their mothers are absent. Adults can also suffer from separation anxiety, as has been found among both men and women deployed in the armed services. During Operation Desert Storm in 1991, many female solders expressed a great deal of separation anxiety both because they had to leave their children but also because of financial worries. All of these worries were even more pronounced among single military mothers.[56]

These anxieties tend to increase the number of military women not willing to re-enlist. In addition, a good number of mothers in the service suffer from psychiatric disorders which make them unfit for combat. Therefore the retention rate for military women is lower than it is for men. Since considerable time and money are needed to train a new recruit, the loss of qualified personnel represents a loss of investment.[57]

In view of these emotionally painful experiences among military mothers, it would seem peculiar that mothers would ever enlist in the services. However, the majority of enlistees come from poor families and therefore are attracted by the benefits which are available to service personnel, such as health insurance, job security, and educational opportunities.

Summary

A number of obstacles face women seeking a military career. These include sexual harassment, which is widespread in all branches of the services, limited physical strength of women soldiers, the belief by some that fighting effectiveness would be compromised by women, the view that all military men and women are "trained killers," contempt for women among many military men, and the antiquated view that military life is an attribute of "manliness."

All of these obstacles were negated by the participation of women in every American war. At first this participation was limited to nurses. However, during the Second World War, numerous women entered the army and joined the WACS or WASPS, including some who flew combat air planes.

After the military academies were opened to women, female participation in the armed forces rose to 15% and resulted in the promotion of some women to the ranks of general and admiral, as well as the appointment of women as commanders of naval ships and army units.

Notes

1. Stephanie Gutmann, Kinder, Gentler Military, (New York: Scribner, 1997):76.

2. Dorothy Schneider and Carl J. Schneider, "Transition to the Military," Educational Horizons, vol. 64, No. 3 (Spring 1966):142–144.

3. Hayes Brown, "Armed Forces Sexual Assault Crisis Reaches New Heights," Think Progress, (May 15, 2013):6.

4. Luis Martinez, "Air Force's Sexual Assault Prevention Officer Charged With Sexual Battery," World New, (May 6, 2013):1–8.

5. Robert Burns, "Army Sexual Assault Prevention Office Coordinator Accused of "Abusive Sexual Contact," Huffington Post, (May 14, 2013):1.

6. Michael Biesecker, "Rapid Fall for Army General Accused of Sex Crimes," Associated Press, (January 6, 2014):1.

7. Micah Zenko and Amelia MacWolf, "Our Military, Our Selves," Foreign Policy, (May 21, 2013):1.

8. No author, Centers for Disease Control, "National Intimate Partner and Sexual Violence Survey," (November 2011).

9. Bonnie S. Fisher, Francis T. Cullen and Michael G. Turner, The Sexual Victimization of College Women, Minnesota Center against Violence and Abuse,(2000).

10.J.J. Knapik, K.I. Reynolds and F. Herman, "Soldier load carriage: Historical, physiological, biomechanical and medical aspects," Military Medicine, vol.169, no.1, (2004):45–55.

11. C. Pandorf, et.al. "Correlates of load carriage and obstacle course performance among women," Work, vol.18, no.2, (2002):179–189.

12. Jack Kenney, "Wanted: Women in Combat for Wars Without End," New American, December 22, 2014):1.

13. Harvey S. Mansfield, "Why a woman can't be more like a man," The Wall Street Journal, November 3, 1997):A22.

14. Eric Schmitt, "First Woman in 6 Decades Gets the Army's Silver Star," The New York Times, (June 17, 2005):A 16.

15. Thomas E. Ricks, Making the Corps, (New York:Simon and Schuster, 1997):289.

16.Department of Defense, "Women in the Military," (12/27/13).

17. Sheryl Stolberg and Melissa Heay, "Harassment is Old Battle for Many Army Women," Los Angeles Times, (November 15, 1996):A22.

18. Charles C. Moskos and John Sibley Butler, All That We Can Be: Black Leadership and Racial Integration the Army Way, (New York:Basic Books, 1996):106.

19. No author, Minerva Quarterly, "Women and the Military," (Spring 1988):2.

20. Susan Zeiger, In Uncle Sam's Service: Women Workers with the American Expeditionary Force, 1917–1919, (Ithaca:Cornell University Press, 1999):104.

21. National American Women's Suffrage Association, "Resolution adopted at the annual convention," Women's Citizen, (April 5, 1919):949.

22. Alicia K. Borlik, "DoD Marks 50th year of Military Women's Integration," DoD News, (June 17 1998):1.

23. Nursing Council on National Defense, American Journal of Nursing, vol.40, (September 1940):1013.

24. No Author, "The Nurse's Contribution to American Victory," American Journal of Nursing, vol.45, (September 1945):683.

25. Lucille Petri, "The U.S. Cadet Nurse Corps: A Summing Up," American Journal of Nursing,vol.45, (1945):1027.

26. Jeanne Holm, Women in the Military, (Navato, CA:Presidio Press, 1992):57.

27. Ibid.:50.

28. Mattie E.. Treadwell, The Women's Army Corps, (Washington DC: Office of the Chief of Military History, 1954).

29. Susan Stamberg, "Female WWII Pilots: The Original Fly Girls," NRP, (March 9, 2010) Morning Edition.

30. Ibid.:13.

31. Air Force Personnel Center, Air Force Military Demographics,":1–6.

32. No author, "First Enlisted Women are Sworn In by Navy," The New York Times, (July 8, 1948):3.

33. Kevin Cahillane, "The Women of West Point", The New York Times Magazine (September 4, 2014)

34. See the catalogues of these service academies.

35. George Foster, "Women Bad for Cadet Morale?" Air Force Times. (May 22, 1974):1.

36. No author, "House Ok's Girl Cadets," Gazette Telegraph, (June 30, 1975):1.

37. Report on Interservice Academy Conference, (October 20, 1975):2.

38. Mary Miller, The Brave Women of the Gulf Wars, (New York: 21st Century Publishers).

39. Mark Thompson, "Female Generals: The Pentagon's First Pair of Four Star Women," Time Magazine, (August 13,2012).

40. Adoratia Purdy, "Dunwoody Relinquishes Command of Army Material Command," Army Magazine, (August 7, 2012).

41. Dan Lamothe, Adm. Michelle Howard becomes First Four Star Woman in Navy History,' The Washington Post, (July 1, 2014):1.

42. No author, "Capt. Kathleen McGrath, Pioneering Warship Commander," The New York Times, (October 1, 2002): Obituaries.

43. Mark Thompson, "The Rise and Fall of a Female Captain Bligh," Time. (March 3, 2010).

44. Daniel F. Burelli, "Women in Combat: Issues for Congress," Washington DC:Congressional Research Service, (May 9, 2013):1.

45. Martin Dempsey, "Allowing women in Combat Strengthens Joint Force," American Forces Press Service, (January 24, 2013).

46. Elizabeth Bumiller and Thom Shanker, "Pentagon Is Set to Lift Combat Ban for Women," The New York Times,

(January 23, 2013):A1.

47. Rasmussen Report, "54% Favor Full Combat Role for Women in Military," http://www.rasmussenreports.com/public_content/politics/general_politics/february_2012/54_favor_full_combat_role_for_women_in_military [accessed June 3, 2015].

48. Office of the Under Secretary of Defense, Personnel and Readiness, "Report to Congress on the Review of Laws Policies and Regulations Restricting the Service of Female Members in the U.S. Armed Forces, (2012):9.

49. Ann Scott Tyson,"The Expanding Role of G.I. Jane," The Christian Science Monitor, (April 3, 2008):1.

50. Rosemary Skraine, Women in Combat, (Santa Barbara, CA:ABC- CIO, 2011):57.

51. No author, "Posthumous honor for fallen Air Force 1st Lt.," Jewish Lights, (January 29, 2010).

52. No author, "Our War Heroes," Chicago Tribune. (September 24, 2006).

53. M.L. Kelley et. al. "Effects of military induced separation on the parenting stress and family functioning of deploying mothers," Military Psychology, vol. 6 (1994):125.

54. R. Cort Kirkwood, "The Military vs. Free Speech," https://www.lewrockwell.com/2003/06/r-cort-kirkwood/the-military-vs-free-speech/ (June 21, 2003), [accessed June 3, 2015].

55.55. D.R. Bey and J. Lange, "Wailing Wives: Women Under Stress," American Journal of Psychiatry, V. 131, (1974):283.

56. Wynd, C.A. and Dziedzicki, R.E. "Hieghtened anxiety in Army reserve nurses anticipating mobilization during Operation Desert Storm, "Military Medicine, vol.157, (1992):610.

57. G.I. Bowen, "Spouse support and the retention intentions of Air Force members," Evaluation and Program Planning, vol. 9, (1986):209.

Chapter Six

Women in Religion

I

The Protestant Experience

There can be little doubt that religion has been an all male stronghold for centuries. Every major religious group in the world was founded by a man, and almost all clergy of every denomination or faith have been men until the middle of the 19th century, when some women were successful in gaining access to the leadership of Protestant congregations in the United States. These women recognized that religion was the only road open to them as a means of defeating the entrenched patriarchy of all the centuries before the present.

Ann Hutchinson was the first American woman to defy the "authorities" in New England in the 17th century. Her "crime" was that she taught the Bible at home to those willing to hear her. This seemed revolutionary to the Puritan clergy, who accused her of witchcraft and expelled her from the Massachusetts Bay Colony because she had questioned the doctrine of original sin and promoted other views which drew larger crowds to her meetings than were available to the orthodox clergy.[1]

The first woman to gain prominence as a religious leader in America was Ann Lee, founder of the United Society of Believers, also known as the Shakers. Together with eight friends, Ann Lee bought Shakerism to America in 1774. Despite immense obstacles, Ann Lee spread the new religion throughout the colonies and later the eastern United States.[2]

Because Ann Lee was illiterate, she left nothing in writing about her life and work. However, her followers have left a number of accounts concerning her religious experiences and her leadership. There are also more modern works describing her life and work.[3]

Ann Lee had devoted followers, but also many enemies. While her followers thought of her as the female Messiah, her detractors viewed her as the devil and a spy for the English. Because of her efforts to win converts, Lee and her followers were beaten, harassed, persecuted and injured as they moved across New England. Ann Lee's personality and her impact on her followers was recorded by numerous personal "testimonies," which later scholars used to develop more than one biography.[4]

Ann Lee died in 1784. Her religion lived after her, and Joseph Meacham became the successor. After her death, her placed in the Shaker community was demeaned, as Meacham claimed that the fourth spirit on earth was not Ann Lee but the community, the other three being Abraham, Moses, and Jesus. Controversy around Ann Lee also stemmed from her assertion that the Trinity was not three men but included women. She viewed God as male and female, and supported equality of the sexes in the Society and therefore in religious practice.[5]

Ann Lee taught her followers that property should be held in common by all believers. Therefore her denomination was called The Society of Believers. This arrangement may well be successful if all members are altruistic and happy to work for the common good. The danger in such an arrangement is that some members may seek to do as little as possible instead of being concerned with the welfare of others.[6]

The Shakers were commanded to remain celibate. Nevertheless, they numbered 1,373 members by 1800, and maintained eleven communities in New York and New England. This had increased to 3,842 members who lived in 21 communities by 1850. These communities were located between Maine and Kentucky.[7]

In 1822, some Shakers settled in an area of Ohio later to become a suburb of Cleveland. This area was then called "The Valley of God's Pleasure," and included farms, a mill, and a school. The families living there were all converts, since Shakers were taught by Ann Lee to be celibate, although she had a husband and children. This policy led to the decline and gradual decimation of the religion.[8]

Mary Baker Eddy was born in New England in 1821 and died in 1910. In 1875, she published Science and Health, a book which has so far sold nine million copies and is still in print in the second decade of the 21st century. The principle argument of this book is that sickness is an illusion which can be cured by prayer alone. Such an argument was far more plausible in the nineteenth century before the rise of modern medicine, at a time when medical knowledge was indeed primitive.[9]

It is fairly evident that Eddy and Lee, as well as Ann Hutchinson in the 17th century, promoted deviant religious beliefs because this satisfied their need for status and power in a male dominated world which reduced women to demented followers of men, thereby closing all other avenues of achievement for women. It was no doubt a means of rebellion and a means of living with the low status assigned to women in Eddy's day that led her to make some of her most extreme claims. Christian Science sought to allow Eddy to dominate at least in the realm of religion and within the limitations provided by her followers.[10]

It needs to be considered that in the nineteenth century, medicine had little prestige because it could hardly help. Medicine was mostly guessing about illness and disease, so that "bleeding" the sick person was common. Few physicians of that day had much knowledge, so that their prestige was low and their profession given little regard, particularly because incompetence was widespread.[11]

Eddy claimed that her "medicine" was safer and more potent than traditional medicine and led to the probability of success. Eddy also wanted to reduce suffering in this life. She became convinced that disease has a mental cause and therefore recommended reading her treatises. She thought that disease and suffering represents human alienation from God. All of these claims were viewed by the clergy as serious threats.[12]

While Christian Science threatened medicine as then practiced, it hardly threatened theology, because it was almost unanimous public opinion that any books or other products of the mind written by a woman were for that reason alone invalid, as women were viewed as incapable of challenging men. In short, it was not Eddy's message but her femaleness that was under attack. It was said that no one who was acquainted with God's Word would listen to a woman. It was claimed that Eddy was suffering from major hysteria connected to menstruation and leading to dementia and hallucinations.[13]

Other enemies of Eddy and her religious convictions claimed that women were intellectually inferior. Professors, philosophers, and writers claimed that women could not deal with abstractions and lacked a sense of reason. Women were also told they could not distinguish lies from truth and therefore could not have any interest in science.[14]

Eddy was accused of being ignorant and illiterate and unable to write an English sentence. It was claimed by "mainline churches" that only fools would be inspired by "Mother" Eddy and that her book Science and Health was a joke.[15]

Nineteenth century men belittled the efforts of women. They trivialized their achievements and claimed that women seeking equality were only interested in power and personal gain, as they envied men and wished to be a man. It was commonly believed that a woman such as Eddy, who promoted unorthodox religious views, had to be insane. Eddy's new religion was called a "cult" and not a religion. Women with ambitions were told they were unpleasant home breakers and were seeking personal glory.[16]

Despite all this criticism, Christian Science survived. This was in part due to Eddy's teaching that God is not responsible for evil in the world and that God could be called Mother as well as Father.

Today the Christian Science church has a membership of about 150,000 worldwide. 100,000 members are Americans. The church publishes The Christian Science Monitor, which has won a number of Pulitzer Prizes for excellence in journalism.[17]

Antoinette Brown (1820–1921) was the first woman to be ordained as a mainstream Protestant minister in the United States. She was principally interested in promoting women's rights. When she was only nine years old, Antoinette began to preach during Sunday meetings. She began to teach school at the age of sixteen and aspired to a degree from Oberlin College in Ohio, which she achieved in 1847. She then sought to enroll in the Oberlin Theological School, but was refused a degree because she was a woman. Having spoken at the National Women's Rights Convention, she was offered a job as minister of the Congregational Church in 1852.[18]

Brown then began to write commentaries on the Bible, with particular reference to the Apostle Paul and his comment that women should not be allowed to speak in church. She wrote that this was not applicable to the 19th century. She then began to speak against slavery and for women's right at a time when women were not normally asked to speak in public.[19]

In 1850 she spoke at the first Women's Rights Convention, and thereby began a speaking tour around the country. This was utterly foreign to women at that time. In 1851, the Congregational Church was the first to give a woman, I.e. Brown, a license to preach. She was offered a position as minister in South Butler, New York. She was ordained by a Methodist minister, Luther Lee.[20]

Shortly after the ordination, she traveled to New York City to attend the World's Temperance Convention as a delegate. She represented two temperance organizations but was not allowed to speak, as no women were allowed to speak. Soon thereafter she resigned her position of minister and married Samuel Blackwell, with whom she had seven children. This was viewed as a failure of a woman to be a minister by the newspapers of that time.[21]

Brown then concentrated her energies entirely on women's liberation. She was not convinced that women would gain equality with men merely by gaining the right to vote. She believed women needed to actively participate in religion and therefore opposed divorce, which other women's rights leaders viewed as a form of liberation from male dominance.

After her marriage, Brown stopped lecturing and began to write. She published The Sexes Throughout Nature in 1875, which argued that the sexes were different but nevertheless equal. She also wrote Studies in General Science, The Island Neighbor, and a collection of poetry.[22]

In 1873, Brown founded the Association for the Advancement of Women. Later she was awarded honorary Master's and Doctor's degrees by Oberlin College. In 1878 she became a Unitarian; she was recognized as a minister of that denomination. She then resumed her lecturing tours.[23]

She died at age 96 in Elizabeth, New Jersey. Her childhood home has been listed in the National Register of Historic Places. In 1975, the United Church of Christ began awarding an annual Antoinette Brown Award to ordained UCC women who "exemplify the contribution that women can make through ordained ministry," etc.[24]

Evangeline Booth (1860–1950) was the daughter of Catherine and William Booth, founders of the Salvation Army in England where Evangeline was born. She began her career as a Christian minister when she was fifteen, selling the Salvation Army's paper The War Cry on the streets of London. At age 21, in 1887, she became an officer of the Salvation Army and was Field Commander for Great Britain from 1888 to 1891. She spent the next five years at officer training, until in 1896 she was sent to America by her father. She was appointed Territorial Commander of the United States, a position she held until 1934.[25]

In 1906, she led a mass meeting in Union Square in New York which raised $12,000 for the relief of the survivors of the San Francisco earthquake. In that year she became a U.S. citizen. Then, in 1917, she led 250 Salvationists to Europe and to the front lines of the First World War. This was viewed with such great admiration at home that the American people contributed $1.3 million in order to clear the Salvation Army's debts resulting from the war.[26]

In 1934, Evangeline was elected General and traveled the world in her cause. She retired in 1939 and then wrote several books, including Toward a Better World and Songs of the Evangel. "Evangeline Booth College" in Atlanta, GA is named after her, as is the Evangeline Booth Lodge in Chicago, which serves the homeless.

On January 1, 2014, the Salvation Army released statistics which showed that the Army had 26,359 officers and 1,150,666 soldiers distributed all over the world.

Ann Hutchinson, Ann Lee, Mary Baker Eddy, Antoinette Brown, and Evangeline Booth were the forerunners of female success in the religious institution. It took many years before their efforts were rewarded with universal acceptance of women in the institution of religion. Indeed, there were women active in numerous Protestant denominations in the 19th century, such as Olympia Brown, who was ordained by the Universalist Church in 1863, and Eleanor Davisson, who became a circuit rider among the Methodists in 1866. These and others were unique and exceptional in their day, so that it was not until the 20th century that it became commonplace for the major denominations among Protestants to employ women in the ministry.[27]

Although there are thousands of female clergy employed in Protestant denominations in the USA, in 2015 this development was only gradually achieved, because most Christians, not only Roman Catholics, believed that only men should have the right to preach. However, here and there individual churches defied that opinion and appointed women to pastoral opportunities. One of these was Addie Davis, who became the first Southern Baptist minister in Durham, North Carolina in 1964 despite the official position of the Southern Baptist Convention to the effect that only men could preach. That ordination was particularly important because the Baptists are the largest Protest denomination in the USA, with twenty-five million members.[28]

Innumerable disputes concerning women in the ministry plagued the Methodist church for years, until the General Conference of the Methodist church decided in 1956 to allow women to be preachers and ministers on an equal basis with men.[29]

The Episcopal Church, related to the Anglican Church in England, first ordained a woman priest in Indianapolis, Indiana. Jacqueline Means became the first woman priest on January 3, 1977, to be followed by many others, including Barbara C. Harris, who became assistant bishop in 1989, and Katherine Jefferts Schori, who became the 26th Presiding Bishop of the Episcopal Church in 2006.

Episcopal priests may be married. It is therefore not surprising that a number of Episcopal priests are converts from Roman Catholicism, which does not allow women to be priests.[30]

II

The Catholic Experience

In September 2013, six months after his election, Pope Francis told a group of journalists that the issue of women priests "is closed." This meant that he agreed with previous popes that women could not be ordained in the Roman Catholic tradition. His predecessor, Pope Benedict XVI (Joseph Ratzinger), had already declared that the ban on women priests is "infallible."[31]

Likewise, the Vatican Congregation for the Doctrine of the Faith had already declared in 1976 that the ordination of women would never be allowed on the grounds that Jesus did not include women among his apostles, that not even his mother was included, and that Jesus was a man. In addition, it is argued that there is an unbroken tradition of an all male priesthood in the church, a view disputed by scholarship.[32]

The word "infallible" means incapable of error. Yet, there is evidence that the early Catholic church did employ women priests. In 1982, Italian professor Giorgio Otranto published "Notes on the Female Priesthood in Antiquity" in Italian. This essay leads to the conclusion that women were not always excluded from the priesthood. Otranto has translated from the Latin some writings of the ninth century bishop of Verelli, Atto. According to Otranto a priest named Ambrose asked Atto how the terms presbyteria and diaconal should be understood. Atto explained that in the early church, women received "sacred orders," as recorded in Romans 16:1, "Commendo nobis Phaebem sororem meanm quae est in minister Ecclesiae quae est Cenchris" or "I commend you to my sister Phoebe who is in the ministry of the church in Cenchris." Bishop Atto of Vercelli evidently claimed that "not only men but also women were ordained dinabantur (Hae quae presbyterae dicebantur praedicandi iubendi vel educendi... officiumsumpserant) or "...as these priests assumed the duty of preaching, ordering and education as well as the office of ministering." These are the three roles of the sacrament of the priesthood.[33]

It should also be noted that the ban on married priests has also been disputed by the Catholic laity for half a century.

In 1979, Pope John Paul II visited Washington, DC. Sister Theresa Kane walked within a few feet of the pope and demanded to know what was the possibility of women being included in the ministry of the church. The Pope did not answer her and an opportunity to deal with this issue was lost. Theresa Kane is president of The Sisters of Mercy, a religious order.[34]

Although women are not called to the priesthood, the Catholic Church has made major adjustments in favor of women in the 21st century. An example of this new attitude was the appointment of Mary Tully as chancellor of the diocese of Portland, Oregon. Tully was the first woman to hold this administrative position. Since then, several other women have also been named chancellors, including Sister Rita Mae Bissonnette of the diocese of Portland, Maine, and Dolores Bernadette Grier, who serves as vice-chancellor in the archdiocese of New York.[35]

Another example of the effort by the Church to include females was the positive vote by the National Conference of Catholic Bishops to allow girls to be altar servers. Heretofore only boys were permitted to be altar boys, Adolf Hitler having been the most famous of all altar boys.[36]

It was not always so. Even during Vatican II, the great ecumenical meeting between 1962 and 1965, there were only 12 lay women and ten religious in attendance, and none were given the right to speak. Since then, women have assumed far more adult roles in the church. In fact, the last forty years have brought about innumerable changes in the lives of Catholic women.[37]

A study of Catholic parishes in America found that 52% of members of Catholic councils were women, that sixty percent of Eucharistic ministers were women, and half of the lectors were also women. Lectors read the scriptures at mass.[38]

The appointments of several Catholic administrators has had a considerable effect on the followers of their own religion. Women now also arrive as administrators of parishes, which has a profound impact on the psyche of young adults. Since Vatican II, women have been allowed to read the scriptures, preach, and distribute communion.[39]

Women have more recently been assigned the role of judges in marriage tribunals, superintendents of schools and directors of Catholic charities. In addition, women have become scripture scholars, canon lawyers, and theologians. These changes were made by Vatican II but also by changes in canon law. The word canon is Greek for "rule" and refers here to a book of church laws. These new rules allow women to be diocesan chancellors, auditors, assessors, defenders of the marriage bond, promoters of the faith, judges of diocesan courts, members of diocesan synods, financial administrative councils, professors, and board members of seminaries.[40]

These changes have allowed Catholic women new opportunities. As more women entered secular organizations such as the Peace Corps, achieved higher education, and made other choices, the number of nuns declined. Alone between 1960 and 1980, a decrease in women entering convents and an increase in the number leaving convents led to a decline in women religious of forty percent.[41]

In 1965, there were at least 165,000 Catholic nuns in the United States. In 2010, the U.S. Catholic Demographic Census reported that then there were only 56,000 nuns in all American seminaries. However, of the 31,000 lay ecclesiastic teachers, eighty percent are women.[42]

The Catholic church has also made an effort to eliminate sexist language from its ceremonies. Thus, the Vatican recently approved a change in the mass. This means that during the "consecration of the host," the text now reads, "for you and for all so that sins may be forgiven," instead of the older version, "for you and for all men," etc. [43]

Birth control practices have traditionally been of concern to the Catholic hierarchy. That tradition has prohibited the use of birth control devices such as condoms, the Lippes loop, the diaphragm, and hormonal and oral contraceptives. This prohibition has been widely ignored by American Catholic women, so that over ninety percent of Catholic women do not think that birth control is a sin. [44]

In 1973, after the Supreme Court ruled in Roe V. Wade that abortion is legal, some Catholics organized Catholics for a Free Choice. This group is based on five tenets. These are, "the moral agency of women; the primacy of informed conscience; the right of Catholics to dissent from noninfallible church teachings; religious freedom and social justice."

These views have led some Catholic women to take steps they regard as legitimate efforts to right the wrongs they believe they have suffered at the hands of the all male clergy. Therefore twelve Catholic women boarded a chartered boat at a Pittsburgh dock in July 2006 and participated in a floating ordination ceremony. This was the first such ceremony in the United States, although similar ceremonies had already taken place in Europe for four years. Those who participated have ordained five bishops and ten priests and deacons. Another eighty Americans had announced their intention of doing the same thing.

These women rely on the evidence that the earliest church did indeed have female priests. Therefore these female priests view themselves eligible to celebrate mass, hear confessions, witness marriages, and baptize. The instigator of this movement is Bridget Meehan, a nun and former television producer.

The Catholic hierarchy rejected this effort in a letter by Bishop Paul S. Loverde which told Ms. Meehan that he feared "for the salvation of her soul." The bishop relied on a statement by Pope John Paul II that "the church has no authority whatsoever to confer priestly ordination on women." The women who participated in these ordinations are regarded by some Catholics as "heretics." [45]

In centuries past, Catholic nuns were a principal segment of American Catholicism. Nuns performed numerous duties, including teaching, but also nursing and assisting priests at numerous tasks. This was possible because the number of nuns in the United States had risen to somewhere between 165,000 and 181,000 in 1965. Then, a constant decline in the numbers of nuns developed, so that now, in 2015, less than 50,000 nuns remain in the American Catholic church. [46]

The American nuns, despite their ever shrinking numbers, have been most vociferous in arguing with the male hierarchy in the church over numerous issues. In 2014, the Leadership Conference of Women Religious, composed of the heads of 80% of U.S. sisters, were under orders to reform. This order was issued by the Congregation for the Doctrine of the Faith and supported by Pope Francis.

There is a strong possibility that the decline in the number of Catholic nuns is largely the result of the reforms introduced at Vatican II and the ascent of all American women in this century.

III

The Jewish Experience

Between 1881 and 1924, two and one half million Jews entered the United States. It was in 1881 that Czar Alexander II was assassinated. His son, Czar Alexander III, blamed the murder on the Jews living in his empire, although no one Jewish had anything to do with that crime. The Russian government organized a nationwide persecution of the Jewish population, including murder, arson of Jewish homes, rape, and expulsions. This kind of treatment was of course common in all of Europe since the fifth century, when Christianity became the official religion of the Roman Empire. From then until our own day, Jews cannot live peacefully in any European country, as attacks on Jewish owned businesses, houses of worship, and individual Jews are common and widespread, from Ireland to the Ukraine, and from Sweden to Italy.[47]

The Jewish migration to American came to an end in 1924, when Congress adopted a quota making immigration from Eastern Europe nearly impossible. There were approximately 400,000 Jews in the country in 1880. These Jews had come from Recife in Brazil and from Germany. The Portuguese speaking Jews were very few, so that German Jewish life predominated in the United States. The wives and daughters of the Portuguese and German Jews had about the same standing as American women generally. In a patriarchal society, they fit in, as women were seldom educated and usually played the role of mother and housekeeper. This was also true of the eastern European Jews, whose families were altogether male centered and who subjugated women within a narrow patriarchy. An example of the treatment of girls among the immigrant Jewish families of the early 20th century is the recollection of Elizabeth Stern. She remembered how her father found her reading Oliver Twist and seized the book, and then told her that her interest in learning English and gaining an education made her an alien to her family. He told her that she was not to go to school beyond an elementary education.[48]

Similar experiences were recorded by Anzia Yesierska, who later became a well known novelist, and Golda Meir, who grew up in Milwaukee and later became the prime minister of Israel.[49]

The eastern European Jews settled mainly in New York and other east coast cities. There they practiced Judaism in a manner that had been common in "the old country" for centuries. Women were viewed as appendages to men and it was universally believed that "only through a man has a woman an existence; only through a man can a woman enter heaven."[50]

This attitude excluded women from participating actively in the religious services which were reserved entirely for men. Women were segregated inside the synagogues (Greek for assembly) in that they were relegated to sitting in the balcony or were seated behind a partition. Women were not allowed to read the Torah or five books of Moses in public nor could they be called to recite a blessing before or after the Torah reading, as was done by men. Jewish practice demanded that ten men, not women, represented a quorum needed for public prayer in which men, but not women, wore a prayer shawl and a skullcap. Instead, women wore a wig to cover their natural hair which was regarded as provocative. Women were not allowed to sing in public, as women's voices were also viewed as sexual provocations. Women could not divorce their husbands, but a man could divorce his wife.[51]

Orthodox Judaism relegated women to the role of housekeeper responsible for the keeping of the Kosher food laws. Women were also enjoined to visit a ritual bath called a Mikvah, but their testimony could not be accepted in court. Sexual behavior was strictly regulated. Men, other than husbands, were not allowed to be alone with a woman. Women's lives were not celebrated in that there was no "bar mitzvah" or confirmation at age 13 for girls, as was the norm for boys. Men even recited a blessing at every daily religious service in which they thanked God for not making them a woman.[52]

These practices were challenged by the Jewish reform movement brought to the United States by some of the 250,000 German Jews who had settled in the U.S. between 1840 and 1900. The Reform Jews called their houses of worship "Temples." They allowed women and men to sit together and they substituted English for Hebrew. The Reform prayer book eliminated such phrases as "I thank God that I am not a woman," as women were counted as part of the quorum of ten Jews at public prayer. Reform Jews also rejected the Jewish food laws. Reform temples initiated sisterhoods. As a result of these changes, many German Jewish families had joined the Reform movement by 1910. Earlier, in 1893, the National Council of Jewish Women was formed. This group of Jewish women made it their task to prevent religious discrimination and persecution. They also sought to assimilate some of the dominant American culture and participated in the early Zionist movement. All of this had enormous consequences for the future of Judaism in America.[53]

Prior to the first part of the 20th century, few Jews of eastern European descent joined the reform movement. It was not until the 1930s that the descendants of the eastern European Jews began to join Reform in large numbers. In addition, American Jews formed a new denomination in the United States called Conservative Judaism. This purely American development gained adherents in the 1880s and grew considerably thereafter. It was promoted by Jews who would no longer accept the orthodox dictums but who also rejected Reform as

imitating Christian methods and values. Conservative Judaism sought to preserve Jewish traditions but also wish to fit into American suburban middle class
life. Thus, men and women were seated together in Conservative synagogues or
temples. Conservative congregations at first continued the prohibition concerning women reading from or handling the Torah. Meanwhile, some Jews rejected
all religion and began to regard themselves as "secular" Jews. The most prominent organization of secular Jews was the Jewish Labor Bund. Bund is German
for association. The secularists accepted women as equals, so that women in
these organizations had more equality with men than women in any of the religious denominations.[54]

By the 1920s, American Jews were largely native born. They developed
numerous organizations, including those devoted to the religious life. While
Orthodoxy continued to demand a lifestyle dominated by religion, Reform and
Conservative Judaism centered on Sabbath and Holy Day observances while
daily activities were altogether secular. As a result, Rabbi Mordecai Kaplan of
the Jewish Theological Seminary wrote that secularism had alienated Jewish
women from Judaism far more than was true of Jewish men.[55]

Yet nothing so alienated the Orthodox Jewish community than the decision
of the Reform movement to allow women to become rabbis. The first woman
ever to become a rabbi was Regina Jonas, who was ordained in Berlin, Germany
in 1935. She was not accepted by any congregation. In 1944, at the age of 42,
she was murdered by the German government.

The first American woman rabbi was Sally Priesand. Ordained by the Hebrew Union College Jewish Institute of Religion in Cincinnati, Ohio in 1972,
she remained an assistant until she became the rabbi of the Monmouth Reform
Temple in New Jersey in 1981. She was a pioneer who has since then been followed by 829 women rabbis of the Reform movement. The Conservative
movement also decided to ordain women, in 1983.[56]

Female Conservative rabbis have had great difficulty in finding employment. There are 300 Conservative women rabbis in the United States. The female enrollment in the Jewish Theological Seminary is larger than that of men,
as 362 women are now enrolled.

A number of women rabbis have achieved considerable prominence since
Sally Priesand became the first of her gender to achieve that status. The first
woman ordained by the Conservative Jewish Theological Seminary was Amy
Elberg, who was ordained in 1985. She earned a B.A. degree in Jewish Studies
from Brandeis University and then studied Talmud at the Jewish Theological
Seminary. She began her career as chaplain at the Methodist Hospital in Indianapolis. After a short stay as assistant rabbi at a synagogue, she moved to California, where she founded the Bay Area Jewish Healing Center in San Francisco
with a view of healing the sick. Subsequently, she married Howard Schwarts,
with whom she had one daughter, and later married Professor Louis Newman.
She then moved to Palo Alto, where she works as pastoral counselor. She teach-

es Jewish healing and Jewish spirituality at several schools, and continues her involvement in services to the sick.[57]

Judith Hauptman has been professor of Talmud and Rabbinics at the Jewish Theological Seminary since 1973. The Talmud (instruction) is a vast compilation of laws and traditions on which post-Biblical Judaism depends. It is exceedingly difficult to interpret and understand, and is studied incessantly by some Jews who spend their lives doing nothing else.

Hauptman holds a Ph.D. in Talmudic studies. Earlier, she was ordained a rabbi after graduating from Barnard College. One of her first efforts was the founding of an outreach project for disaffected Jews. She also organized walk-in services on the high holy days and presides over Passover "seders" or ritual dinners.

In her role of professor, she has written on issues of Talmudic law and on women's issues. In the 1970s, she lobbied for the egalitarianism in Jewish life.[58]

Naomi Levy was ordained a rabbi at the Jewish Theological Seminary in 1989. She became the first female congregational rabbi on the West Coast, where she stayed for seven years. She wrote a book To Begin Again which deals with the murder of her father in an armed robbery. In 2004, she founded an outreach service for Jews no longer interested in the traditional Jewish services. She leads social action programs in the Los Angeles area and supports Friday night services for any Jews willing to attend. These draw large crowds.

Levy has been featured on NBC's show Today, on Oprah, and in Parade Magazine. She is a member of the faculty at the Wexler Heritage Foundation at the Academy of Jewish Religion. Her third book, Hope Will Find You, was published in 2011. This deals with her daughter's very dangerous illness.Levy is married to Robert Eshman, editor of The Jewish Journal of Greater Los Angeles.

In March of 2015, Denise Eger became the president of the Central Conference of American Rabbis. This is the organization of American Reform rabbis. Reform has about 1.1 million adherents. The Central Conference is the oldest rabbinical organization in North Amerca. Eger is the third woman and also the first lesbian to hold that position.

Eger is a native of Memphis, Tennessee. In 1982 she graduated from the University of Southern California with a degree in religion. In 1985 she earned a master's degree from the Hebrew Union College / Jewish Institute of Religion and went on to pursue rabbinic studies. Ordained in 1988, she became a full time rabbi at a Los Angeles synagogue. This congregation was then the first lesbian and homosexual synagogue recognized by the Reform movement. In 1992, she and thirty-five others founded Congregation Kol Ami, a Hebrew term for "all my people."

Thereafter, Eger presided over the Women's Rabbinical Network, and later became president of the Pacific Association of Reform Rabbis. She also founded the Religion and Faith Council and worked actively for California Faith for

Equality. She was active in helping HIV / AIDS patients, and has authored numerous articles in such journals as Torah Queries and Twice Blessed.[59]

Because the number of Afro-American Jews is so small, it is surprising that a black woman has become a rabbi. She is Alysa Stanton, who was ordained in 2009 by the Hebrew Union College / Jewish Institute of Religion. She became the rabbi of a synagogue in Greenville, South Carolina, and stayed two years.[60]

In view of the developments in Judaism which favor the equality, if not the ascendancy of women in Reform and Conservative congregations, it would seem incongruous that some American Jewish women prefer to join the Jewish Orthodox community. Yet, this is the case for some women who reject all secular "liberation" movements on the grounds that in their view these movements compromise responsibility to the family. Many of these women did at one time experiment with various "new age" groups such as transcendental meditation and others, and felt that these groups did not furnish them with a sense of security and belonging which Orthodox Judaism seemed to provide. These women had repeatedly met men who were unable to make any lasting commitment, while such commitment is almost universal in Jewish orthodoxy. These women also reject the notion of women's equality with men, which seems to them as an attempt to discard the differences between the sexes. Because orthodoxy celebrates the family, those women already attuned to elevate family above all other values are attracted to Orthodox Judaism.[61] Among the most fundamentalist Jews, it is believed that women are responsible for the coming of the Messiah. Orthodoxy demands that women follow the "purity laws," including ritual bathing. Every Jewish community supports a ritual bath, which cleanses women of the impurities associated with menstruation. Despite these beliefs, most Orthodox women work and hold husbands responsible for some domestic activity. Orthodox women prefer concrete, absolute rules over total self determination. These women ignore the Orthodox beliefs that only men can perform the Jewish rituals and believe that they are equal to men.

Summary

Beginning with Ann Hutchinson and continuing with Ann Lee and Mary Baker Eddy, Antoinette Brown, Evangeline Booth, and Addie Davis, American women gradually overcame the religious patriarchy common in Christian and Jewish religious establishments.

American Catholic women have also benefitted from the American drive for gender equality, despite the refusal of the hierarchy to permit women to enter the priesthood. Women have been appointed to numerous important positions in Catholic education, in the administration of important institutions, and in numerous influential decision-making bodies.

Likewise, American Jews have accepted women as rabbis, teachers, administrators, and scholars within the Reform and Conservative denominations.

Notes

1. Selma R. Williams, Divine Rebel: The Life of Ann Marbury Hutchinson, (New York: Holt, Rinehart and Winston, 1981).

2. Nardi Campion, Ann the Word: The Life of Mother Ann Lee, Founder of the Shakers (Boston: Little Brown, 1976).

3. Richard Francis, Ann the Word: The Story of Ann Lee (New York: Arcade Publishing Co., 2000).

4. Stephen Marini, "A New View of Mother Ann Lee and the Rise of American Shakerism," Shaker Quarterly, vol. 18, (1990).

5. Marjorie Proctor Smith, "Who do you say I am? Mother Lee as Christ," Locating the Shakers, (Exeter, England: University of Exeter Press, 1990).

6. John Bonin and Louis Putterman, Economics of Cooperation and the Labour Managed Economy, (London: Routledge, 2001).

7. William S. Bainbridge, "Shaker Communities," Journal for the Scientific Study of Religion, vol. 49, no. 1, (2010).

8. Glendyne Wegland, "Our Shaker Ancestors," New England Ancestors, vol. 7, no. 5–6, (2006):21.

9. Rodney Stark, "The Rise and Fall of Christian Science," Journal of Contemporary Religion, vol. 12, no. 2 (1998):189–214.

10. Margery Fox, "Protest in Piety: Christian Science Revisted," International Journal of Women's Studies, vol. 1 (July –August 1978):401.

11. Everett T. Tomlinson, "The Decline of the Ministry," World's Work, New York, vol. 8 (December 1904):563.

12. Andrew F. Underhill, Valued Observations to So-called Christian Science, (Yonkers, NY: Arlington Chemical, 1902):30–31.

13. J.P. Mobius, "The Physiological Mental Weakness of Women and the Lower Races," Alienist and Neurologist, vol. 22 (October 1901):624.

14. Paul Siegvold, The Ideal American Lady, (New York: Putnam's, 1893):77.

15. Frank Crane, "Christian Science and Insanity," Methodist Review, vol. 91 (May 1909):447.

16. John Halperin, "Trollope and Feminism," South Atlantic Quarterly, vol. 77 (Spring 1978):181.

17. B.A. Robinson, "Ontario Consultants on Religious Tolerance," July 15, 2011.

18. James T. White, "Blackwell, Antoinette Louise Brown," The National Cyclopedia of American Biography.

19. Carol Lasser, "Blackwell, Antoinette Louisa Brown," American National Biography Online, http://www.anb.org/articles/15/15–00064.html, [accessed April 21, 2015].

20. Susan Hill Lindley, You Have Stepped Out of Your Place, (Louisville, Kentucky: Westminster John Knox Press, 1996):122.

21. No author, "Rev. Antoinette Brown seems to have made a failure of her first pastorate," Boston Investigator, (May 6, 1857), 19th Century US Newspapers via Gale Group, http://infotrac.galegroup.com.

22. No author, "Blackwell, Antoinette Louise Brown," in The National Encyclopedia of American Biography, vol. 19 (New York: James T. White & Co., 1941):129.

23. Nickolas C. Burckel, "Oberlin College," Handbook of American Women's History, Thousand Oaks, CA (Sage Publications, 2000):407.

24. Ibid:407

25. Edward T. James, Janet James and Paul Boyer, Notable American Women: A Biographical Dictionary (Cambridge, MA: Harvard University Press, 1971).

26. Ibid.

27. Bruce R. Robinson, "When Churches Started to Ordain Women," Ontario Consultants on Religious Tolerance, (March 29, 2011).

28. Religious News Service, "First Female Southern Baptist Preacher Dies," (December 17, 2005).

29. Higher Education & Ministry, http://www.gbhem.org/clergy/clergywomen/history, (accessed April 24, 2015).

30. No author, "Woman Episcopal Priest Celebrates Communion," The New York Times, (January 3, 1977):14.

31. Robert McClory, "Pope Francis and Women's Ordination," National Catholic Reporter, (September 16, 2013):1.

32. Vatican Congregation for the Doctrine of the Faith, "Declaration on the Question of the Admission of Women to the Priesthood," in Rosemary Radford Ruether, Ed., Women-Church: Theology and Practice (San Francisco: Harper & Row, 1986):129.

33. Mary Ann Rossi, "Priesthood, Precedent and Prejudice," Journal of Feminist Studies in Religion, vol. 7, no. 1, (Spring 1991):73.

34. Ann Goldman, "The Papal Visit: Nun Still Keeps the Faith On Larger Women's Role," The New York Times, (September 18, 1987):1.

35. Ari L. Goldman, "Go-Ahead for Altar Girls," The New York Times, (July 2, 1994):Religion Notes.

36. Ibid:1.

37. Helen Ebaugh and Paul Ritterband, "Education and the Exodus from Convents," Sociological Analysis, vol. 39, (1978):256–264.

38. David Lege and Thomas A. Trozzolo, "Who Participates in Local Church Communities?" Origins, V. 15, 1985:49–57.

39. Ibid:56–57.

40. Maria Augusta Neal, "Women in Religious Symbolism and Organization," Sociological Inquiry, vol. 49 (1979):218.

41. Ibid:19.

42. U.S. Catholic Demographic Census.

43. Origins (May 2, 1985).

44. Andrew M. Greeley, Angry Catholic Women, Chicago: Thomas More Press, (1985):216–217.

45. Michelle Boorstein, "Reclaiming the Feminie Spirit in the Catholic Priesthood," The Washington Post, (July 30, 2006):1

46. Allie Conti, "The State of the Aging Sisters," Vice, (July 22, 2013).

47. Max L. Margolis and Alexander Marx, A History of the Jewish People, (Philadelphia: The Jewish Publication Society, 1960):721–722.

48. Irving Howe, World of Our Fathers, (New York: Harcourt, Brace, Jovanovich, 1976):267.

49. Ibid:268.

50. Alice Kessler Harris, Bread Givers, (New York: George Braziller, 1975):VI.

51. Ann Lapidus Lerner, "Who Has Not Made Me a Woman: The Movement for Equal Rights for Women in American Jewry," American Jewish Yearbook, (1977):8.

52. Ibid:8.

53. Rebecca Kohut, "Jewish Women's Organizations in the United States," American Jewish Yearbook, 1931–1932, (Philadelphia: Jewish Publication Society, 1931), vol. 33:175.

54. Alice Kesller Harris, "Organizing the Unorganizable: The Jewish Women and their Union," Labor History, (Winter 1976):17.

55. Mordecai Kaplan, "What the American Jewish Woman Can Do for Adult Jewish Education," Jewish Education, vol. 4 (October-December 1932):139–140.

56. Steven M. Cohen, "American Jewish Feminism: A Study in Conflict and Compromises," American Behavioral Scientist, vol. 23, no. 4, (1980):519.

57. Raye T. Katz, "Exploring the Link Between Womanhood and the Rabbinate," Lilith, vol. 14, (1985–1986):20–21.

58. Rosemary Keller, Rosemary Radford Ruether and Marie Canton, Encyclopedia of Women and Religion, (Indianapolis, IN: Indiana University Press, 2006).

59. Julie Greenbaum, "Glass Ceiling Twice Shattered at Board of Rabbis," The Jewish Journal of Greater Los Angeles, (May 6, 2009).

60. David Kaufman, "Introducing America's First Black Female Rabbi," Time, (June 6, 2009).

61. Dorothy Kaufman, "Women Who Return to Orthodox Judaism," Journal of Marriage and the Family, vol. 47, (1985):543.

Chapter Seven

Women in Law Enforcement and Corrections

I

Prior to the nineteenth century there were no women in any police force in the United States. Then, in 1845 two women were appointed to the New York City police department. They were called police matrons and were employed to deal with women and girls held in police custody. A number of other cities followed this example.[1]

The first policewoman ever appointed in this country was Mrs. Marie Owens, who, for thirty years beginning in 1893, dealt with women and children in court and police lockups. In 1905, in Portland, Oregon, Mrs. Lois Baldwin was appointed to the police force with power over women and girls deemed to live in undesirable conditions and under deviant influences. Finally, in 1910, the first full time regular policewoman, Mrs. Alice Wells, was appointed in Los Angeles. She was employed in supervising dance halls, skating rinks, penny arcades, movies, and any other sites dealing with public amusements. She also warned against billboard displays regarded as obnoxious, searched for missing persons, and talked to women seeking the help of the police department.[2]

By 1915 there were a sufficient number of women employed in American police departments that they founded The National Association of Police Women. This organization disbanded in 1932 for lack of money.[3]

The majority of women so employed were assigned to deal with children accused of juvenile delinquency. In addition, women police were concerned with neglected children and with women engaged in prostitution. In some towns and cities, women also performed traffic control duties.

During World War I, women were used as police in military training camps with a view of keeping prostitutes away from the camps and returning girls to their homes. Consequently more and more police departments employed women, so that by 1920 over two hundred police departments employed women.

In recognition of these developments, the International Association of Chiefs of Police passed a resolution at their 1922 convention stating that women were essential to the then modern police departments. This recognition of women as members of the police profession was in part promoted by the increasing participation of women in public affairs as a consequence of the success of the suffragettes, so that in 1920, women finally voted in federal elections. Nevertheless, the majority of policemen viewed female police as social workers and not true police professionals. Many police chiefs held women in contempt and assured themselves that women as police were only a temporary fad. Police then and now were interested in penalizing the citizens and not in preventing crimes.

In 1930, women were first employed on a state level by Massachusetts to be followed almost at once by Connecticut and Michigan.

In 1945, Techniques in Law Enforcement was published. This publication advised that policewomen should be college graduates with a social work background and that they should have a "balanced" personality. This meant that policewomen were advised not to seem mannish or excessively feminine.[4]

In 1953, Evabel Tenny advised policewomen to be dignified. She further wrote that policewomen should we well dressed and command respect by appearing attractive, alert, and interested in the welfare of others without becoming too sentimental.[5]

Another publication concerning women in policing is Women in Law Enforcement by Mary Anderson, a police sergeant in Portland, Oregon. Anderson complains about sexism in police departments in which there is often only one woman member. This was written in 1973 when there were indeed few women in police work. That had changed dramatically by 2014, when the Bureau of Labor Statistics reported that 12.5%, or 82,000 of 680,000 American police officers, are women.[6]

No doubt this increase in the participation of women in policing was promoted in part by the civil rights movement of the 1960's, which resulted in the passage of the Civil Rights Act of 1964, which Congress amended in 1972 prohibiting discrimination based on gender in public as well as private employment. In 1973, the Crime Control Act, which specified that sex discrimination by law enforcement agencies is prohibited, was passed by Congress. In addition, the act required that such agencies, I.e. police departments, must set up women's equal opportunity plans.[7]

As a result of these laws, women have been employed on patrol duty, as detectives and as investigators., in traffic control and as administrators. Beginning in 1971, women were given the right to carry weapons, so that they are now also employed as security guards and F.B.I. agents.[8]

The employment of women police is not limited to the United States. In Tokyo, Japan, 850 policewomen are working in the traffic department, in England, women are part of the detective force in Scotland Yard, the London police, and in Israel, ninety percent of traffic police are women. Likewise, Sweden, Norway, Australia, New Zealand, and Austria employ women police.[9]

Because women police are now used extensively, it is of interest to note why women want to become police officers. One reason is to call attention to women victimized by assault and rape. It had been common for all male police departments to be inactive with reference to women's complaints regarding violence.[10]

Women are motivated to join police because they seek to help others. This is demonstrated by the evidence that 37 percent of women who join police forces were formerly employed in helping professions such as social work, nursing, and teaching.[11]

Policemen have traditionally been opposed to the participation of women. That has changed somewhat in the last few years as more and more women were employed. Nevertheless, many policemen still believe that women were not welcome on patrol duty because they were viewed as less capable as men to deal with dangerous situations. More objective studies have shown that women are as capable as men as police officers although there are some differences in the emphasis placed on various situations. This means that men are more capable of handling violence than are women, although that estimate is not absolute.

Policewomen began to attain equality with men in the 1970's. This came about because laws demanded this and also because "affirmative action" secured the rights of women and minorities. [12]

Despite these developments, there are those who claim that discrimination against policewomen has continued. Nevertheless, it appears that affirmative action has not only increased the number of women police since the 1970's but has also allowed women to achieve promotions in the rigid hierarchy of police employment. In 1978, women were only 1% of all supervisors. By 1986 women had become 3.8% of supervisors, a number which increased to 15.9% in 2014. [13]

Women in urban police departments participate in patrol work with men and gradually become integrated into the informal subculture of the occupation. Women police, like male police, are in regular contact with those who work their shift. Police work three shifts every day and therefore learn to know each other well. They banter before each shift, meet for coffee, engage in conversation, back each other up during their shift, and finally deposit their paperwork with the sergeant on duty. [14]

This picture appears to promote the view that women and men police share the same stress under the same work conditions. However, it appears that women police have to deal with more stress than male police because of work-home conflict and because they work in a male dominated environment. These difficulties concern all women who work outside the home despite the more recent gender role changes. Even now, in 2015, women more often than men contribute to maintaining the home and dealing with children. Recent studies have shown that among working women, including female police, 64% of women put 15 hours or more into child care per week. Only 39% of men spend 15 hours of their time toward child care. Even in families in which men share some of the domestic work, women still do two-thirds of the daily chores such as cooking and cleaning. Yet, policewomen and others are under stress to perform as competently as men. [15]

Because police work occurs in a male dominated environment, women police encounter a number of policemen who do not want women on the job and who let their displeasure be known. The percentage of men with such an attitude may be declining. Sexual harassment and other forms of discrimination lead women to leave the police force, as does excessive scrutiny by male colleagues who seek to make women police feel unwanted. Policing is always a stressful job and becomes more so if one's colleagues increase the discomfort by creating a negative work environment.

Women in any police organization are few in number and therefore become highly visible token members. They experience performance pressure because they lack anonymity, as they are viewed as representative of all women. Men enjoy relative anonymity because of their large numbers, representing only themselves. This situation faces women in all occupations in which they are gendered newcomers and few in numbers. All of this began in the 1970's, because there were hardly any sworn women in any police department before then. The few who did have police appointments in earlier years worked with women and children exclusively and were not seen as competing with men. Thus, in 1970, less than one percent of sworn police were women, in 1990 about 11 percent were women, and in 2015 this rose to 13%.

There can be little doubt that women seeking to join a police force are attracted by the authority this allows them. Few Americans have the opportunity to exert power over other citizens. Yet, that opportunity is available to police and prison guards, and makes such work most attractive. John Dalberg, Lord Acton, wrote "power corrupts and absolute power corrupts absolutely." Power is a mighty aphrodisiac hardly available to the average American citizen. But those who wear the police uniform can demand instant obedience to their every command, legal or not. That attracts women as well as men, but has led to extensive violence between citizens and law enforcement.

The best paying jobs in policing are those of state troopers. The New York State Police is a good example of this nationwide method of supervising America's throughways. The New York State Police was organized in 1917 as the result of a campaign led by two women, Moyca Newell and Katherine Mayo. Yet it was 1956 when the first female recruits were admitted to the NYSP academy. It took another eighteen years before four women were sworn in 1974 as New York State troopers. In 2015 four hundred women were New York state troopers out of a contingent of over 4,600 men and women. The salaries of state troopers are higher than is true of municipal police. The starting salary for a New York state trooper is $66,905, which increases to over $71 thousand in the second year of employment. In New Jersey, the starting salary is $62,403, which increases to over $69 thousand in the second year. In Alaska, state troopers earn $54,420 to start without a degree and $56,460 with a bachelor's degree. The lowest pay for state troopers is in New Hampshire, where first year troopers earn only $46,307.04.[16]

The state police are responsible for patrolling the state highway system. They also protect state facilities and support rural law enforcement. Except for New Jersey and a few other states, no degree is required to join the state troopers. Usually sixty hours of college are required; that requirement is equal to an associate's diploma from a two year junior college. Upon appointment, state troopers attend a state police academy lasting between four and six months. The new recruit lives in a dormitory on the academy campus for three months. Patrol and investigative techniques are the curriculum, together with firearms training, self-defense, driving, water safety, and constitutional and criminal law. In addition, extensive physical training is required, including times runs and swims.[17]

Among women serving in the New York State Police are some who have achieved administrative standing. One of these is "Colonel" Patricia M. Groeber. She is deputy superintendent in division headquarters, where she serves as field commander. It is notable that the state police imitate the military by labeling employees with military ranks and insignia. These practices serve the U.S. military establishment in face of armed enemies. Evidently, the state police, and other police departments, view American citizens as their enemy.

Damais Abrams-Jones, stationed in New York City, is an investigator with the New York State Police, as is Kelly Strack, who deals with forensic identification. This deals with the collection and preservation of physical evidence at a crime scene.

Technical sergeant Kathy Humphries is an aviator for the NYSP aviation unit. She participates in medical evacuation search and rescue operations, scuba dives, and transport for state officials.

Women are also found in the military police. For example, the 221st Military Police Detachment is commanded by Captain Samantha Hoxha. Sgt. Selene Savarina is also a member of the 221. Also included is Spc. Adrianna Williamson, who agrees with other women in her company that women have to work twice as hard as men. Women military police deal with detainees and with convoy operations, base security, and host nations' mentors. Women military police also handle dogs who act as explosive detectors. The military police also employs a SWAT team called a Special Reaction Team. That too includes women.[18]

Women have also succeeded working for the F.B.I. According to F.B.I. male veterans, few women ever apply to work for the F.B.I. because women believe they need to "smash the doors down" or use other physically violent methods. In fact, the F.B.I. seeks candidates with backgrounds in accounting, computer science, engineering, and foreign languages. There are about 12,000 F.B.I. agents, of whom only 2,100 are women. Agents earn between $54,000 and $58,000 annually. Among the secretarial support staff, however, there are nearly 16,000 employees, of whom sixty-seven percent are women.

Women are sought after as agents because F.B.I. management believes that women are more efficient in moving between different ways of relating to the world. Women are also credited with having more verbal fluency and verbal memory skills than men. Women police are responsible for fewer lawsuits than men, and appear more competent in dealing with hostage negotiations.[19]

II

Despite numerous obstacles related to the public prejudice against women in police work, some women succeeded in becoming leaders in the profession as early as 1924, when Hannah C. Saunders was elected sheriff of Burnett County in Wisconsin to replace her husband, outgoing sheriff Charles. Since then, Wisconsin has sworn in almost 50 women sheriffs. Texas is the only other state which has had a sizable number of women sheriffs. In Texas, the majority of women so appointed were the widows of former sheriffs. In Wisconsin this was not the case. Here almost all women sheriffs were elected on their own merits.[20]

Sheriffs are the chief law enforcement officers in any American county. In Wisconsin, voters determined that sheriffs could not succeed themselves and were therefore limited to one term. In 1929, this law was changed and sheriffs were then allowed to serve two consecutive terms. Nevertheless, those who held these positions wanted to stay in office much longer. They therefore appointed their wives as undersheriffs. At the conclusion of their two terms in office, the wives ran for sheriff and appointed the husbands undersheriffs. Consequently the husband assumed the sheriff's position when his wife had served two terms. This arrangement produced numerous female sheriffs, including Ruth Atkinson, Dolores Lein, Dorothy Spencer, Ella Reinel, Gloria Bridenhagen, and numerous others.[21]

In 2001 the National Center for Women and Policing surveyed the largest municipal and state law enforcement agencies in the United States and discovered that then women made up only 12.2 % of all police employees.[22]

The F.B.I. Uniform Crime Report recorded that in 2003 only 11.4% of police were women. At that time the majority of police agencies did not employ any women. Now women are about 12% to 13% of all police, of whom 7.3% have risen to command posts. There are a number of local police agencies that have promoted women into higher ranks. Meanwhile the Federal agencies such as the FBI and the Secret Service have also employed women. In fact, the first female director of the Secret Service was Julia Pierson, who was appointed in March of 2013. Her job was to protect the president, the vice president, and their families. Pierson had thirty years of experience but was forced to resign on October 2, 2014, after only eighteen months, because during her short term as director, an agent passed out drunk in a hallway of the White House, an intruder breached the White House, and a contractor with a criminal record rode on an elevator with President Obama while carrying a gun in his pocket.[23]

Pierson is not the only woman to have become police chief. In fact, several women have succeeded in heading police departments, including Elizabeth Bondurant, who was the chief In Plainsboro, New Jersey, where she joined the police department in 1983. She became chief in 2007 while also teaching a number of courses at Monroe County Community College.[24]

Betsy Gilardi became the chief of police in Dobbs Ferry, New York in August of 2007. The divorced mother of two children, she is the only woman in the department where she has served for twenty-two years.[25]

The first woman chief of police in the United States was Penny Harrington. She was appointed chief of the Portland, Oregon police department in 1985. She founded "The National Center for Women and Policing" before she left for Los Angeles, where she worked as a consultant dealing with a number of police issues. Harrington resigned after only six months in office because her husband had alerted a suspect in a major cocaine case.[26]

In 1994, Beverly Harvard was appointed chief of the Atlanta, GA police department. She thereby became one of three women to head a police department of a large American city. A graduate of Morris Brown College in Atlanta, she joined the police force twenty-one years earlier. Later she earned a master's degree in public administration from Georgia Tech University.[27]

In January 1990, Elizabeth Watson was named police chief in Houston, Texas. She was appointed by the woman mayor of Houston, Kathryn Whitmire. Watson comes from a family of police officers. Her grandfather, her sister, her husband and several cousins all served as police officers. She is a graduate of Texas Tech University in psychology. She joined the police force in 1972. Watson remained in Houston only two years and then headed the Austin, Texas, force for five years before retiring.[28]

III

Probation and parole have also traditionally been a men only form of employment. The few women who were appointed to these positions before the 1970's dealt only with women probationers, who were very few. Indeed, rehabilitation has been the announced objective of both probation and parole. Yet, custody, surveillance and control have been the major focus of the profession. As treatment has slowly entered the area of concern, women have been given a greater opportunity to participate in the supervision of men. It was 1949 when the first female parole officer was appointed in Washington State to deal with female offenders. Tradition had precluded the mere idea of allowing women to supervise men. This changed when the openings for positions as probation and parole officers could not be filled by a sufficient number of male applicants, even as women officers had to travel considerable distances to visit the few probationers and parolees on their caseloads.

In the 1960's a number of qualified women applied to become probation officers, but were not considered until it became evident that women could deal with male offenders just as women had for years dealt with male recipients of public assistance.[29]

The anxiety concerning male offenders conducting themselves in an aggrieve fashion towards female probation officers may well be unjustified. There are, however, circumstances which lead women officers to become sexually involved with probationers. One such example, but not the only one, concerns Jennifer Corquin, a married woman, who became enamored with Jack Logan, a parolee under her supervision. Logan had been convicted of murder. After his release, he and Corquin began "an affair," leading them to visit bars and hotels together until they were both arrested and jailed.[30]

As a consequence of these developments, women are now more numerous among probation and parole officers than men, occupying 52.5% of positions in these occupations.[31]

Corrections was for centuries a purely male occupation because it was believed that the violence and unpredictability of male prisons made such work unsuitable for women. Yet, the last fifty years have seen the slow infiltration of women into men's prisons. This was made possible because Title VII of the Civil Rights Act of 1964 as amended in 1972 guaranteed the right of women to serve as guards and administrators in men's prisons. In addition, the 1977 Supreme Court decision in Dothard V. Rawlinson defeated the height and weight requirements imposed on prison guards in Alabama. According to those restrictions, an applicant had to be at least 5'2" tall and weigh 120lbs. [32] As a result, there are about 43,000 women prison guards in the U.S. today (2015). Female prisons have always been under the jurisdiction of women guards. Since women prisoners are few, opportunities for women in corrections were severely limited. These opportunities are burdened by the resentment many male officers exhibit towards women in an all male institution, and additionally become complicated by the sexual harassment imposed on women officers by both the male staff and the prisoners.[33]

Crouch and Alpert report that the primary reason women correctional officers take the job is an interest in human science work or in inmate rehabilitation. Fifty-five percent of those studied by these researchers held that view. Salary was mentioned by only 13% of women taking a job as correctional officers. Among male officers, 23% indicated that human service work was the first reason for becoming prison guards and salary ranked at eight percent. Attitudes towards inmates were also analyzed by researchers, with the result that male and female prison guards did not differ significantly in sympathy for the prisoners.[34]

Although women have had a good deal of success as prison guards in male institutions, many Americans still question whether women can perform these tasks. Prison guard jobs were for so long reserved only for men that it seems incongruous that women should be in a position of authority over men. According to Max Weber, those working for entrenched bureaucracies will behave in a similar manner no matter what their individual characteristics. According to that theory, gender should make no difference in the manner in which the position of prison guard is performed.[35]

A number of students of behavior have found that women who work in traditionally male jobs will gradually assume male behavior. These findings are in line with the discovery that social structure heavily shapes the opinions and conduct of individuals who adapt to their environment.[36]

Women prison guards are often resented by male guards and administrators, who deliberately withhold information from women guards. Sexual harassment from male guards is very common. And many women guards wonder whether male guards would back them up if needed. This means that women guards often lack the support that is essential in doing the job. This leads some women guards to form alliances with inmates, who then voluntarily comply with orders.[37]

Such compliance is limited because there are female–male interactions which create embarrassment and anxiety in the prisoners. One of these is the strip-search conducted regularly in prisons seeking to discover whether the inmate has drugs and/or weapons in his underwear or on his body. Such a search by a female guard led a prisoner to claim in court that jail officials had violated his rights by having a female guard trainee search inside his shorts and pat down his genitals. The Ninth U.S. Circuit Court of Appeals in San Francisco ruled that the search was constitutional and justified. The judge, Sandra Ikuta, speaking for the majority, granted that the search was invasive and embarrassing. She wrote that the prison had allowed female guards to observe naked prisoners and that a ban on such activities would significantly limit the usefulness of female guards.[38]

The female prison guard behavior largely reflects female-male relationships outside of prison, such as being motherly and supportive. This works for women prison guards, as men respond by being protective, which is male behavior in general. Women have a calming effect on male prisoners, so that the argument that women guards present a danger during violent events in a prison is offset by the reduction of such events when women are present. It is therefore reasonable to suggest that prison violence and security issues would be reduced if men adopted the strategies that have been so successful when used by women.[39]

It would be remarkable if the presence of women guards in male institutions did not lead to some sexual encounters. This is illustrated by the conduct of Tevon White, who developed a harem of women correctional officers while in the Baltimore, MD city jail. He impregnated four officers, with whom he had sex in a closet while officers watched outside. The four women gave birth to White's children. Boss of a gang calling itself the Black Guerilla Family, his female followers smuggled drugs and other items into the jail for him. Thirteen others were also indicted after these activities were discovered.[40]

A male prisoner, Jang Li Delgado Galban, sued Washington County, Oregon on the grounds that two female prison guards had sex with him while in prison for second degree assault. According to the district attorney, a female guard, Jill Curry, unlocked Galban's cell on 13 occasions and then had sex with him in a closet. Likewise, Brett Robinson, also a female guard, pleaded guilty to having sex with Galban. Both women were sentenced to four years in jail. Robinson also opened Galban's cell after he sent her a sexually explicit note, which she answered with a love letter.[41]

Rebecca Zong, a prison guard at the State Correctional Institution at Rockwell, PA, was charged with having had sex with a prisoner after writing him a sexually explicit note. She then conducted the sexual encounter in the chapel of the prison. She has been charged with sexual assault although the sex was consensual, because Pennsylvania law regards all sexual relations between guards and inmates as coerced.[42]

On June 12, 2015 Joyce Mitchell was arrested by New York State police for aiding two convicted killers to escape from the Dannemora N.Y. Clinton Correctional Facility on June 6, 2015. Davod Sweat and Richard Matt used power tools to gain their freedom. No evidence exists to connect Mitchell with these tools although she was charged with bringing "contraband" into the prison.[43]

Once women were admitted to the position of prison guard, it was inevitable that a woman would become a warden at a major penal institution. Thus, in April of 2008, Lisa Hollingsworth became the first female warden of the United States Penitentiary at Marion, Illinois. That medium security facility had 910 inmates, and the minimum security facility at that same location had a population of 290 inmates. At the time of her appointment, Hollingsworth oversaw both facilities. She had 23 years' experience with the Bureau of Prisons, where she started as a college intern major in criminal justice. She began her career working in the Washington, DC office of the Federal Bureau of Prisons. She then went to the Federal Correctional Institution at Bastrop, Texas, where she worked with case management staff and later as a case manager. This appointment allowed her to establish programs to deal with the educational needs of prisoners, and find work assignments for them while in prison and halfway houses once released. She also placed prisoners in drug and anger management programs.[44]

In March, 2010, Terri Gonzalez became the warden of the California Men's Colony, a medium-minimum security prison in San Luis Obispo. The facility has 2,200 employees and 6,400 inmates. Gonzalez began her career as a correctional officer in 1988. Later she became a correctional lieutenant, then an employee relations officer, and thereafter a correctional captain. That led to a position with the California Standard Review Board before she became warden. The job includes dealing with a $153 million budget spent largely on employees' payroll and upkeep of the buildings.[45] Gonzalez has one child with her ex-husband.

Kate Butler is the warden at the Menard Correctional Facility in Chester, Illinois, established in 1878. That prison houses 3,700 men, of whom half have been convicted of murder. Another quarter have been convicted of violent offenses such as rape, kidnapping, and armed robbery. Sixty-five percent will be in prison for life. The prison has experienced three inmate murders and had so much violence that two thirds of 2012 were spent on lockdowns. This has been greatly reduced, as warden Butler increased access to the law library and the grievance system.

Butler oversees 900 employees, of whom 180 are women. Butler was for two years the director of programs at the prison after eighteen years as a correctional officer. As warden, she answers all telephone calls by relatives of inmates. She also allows prisoners to serve as transition facilitators for new inmates, and others as assisted living aides for the aged prisoners.

It is apparent that Kim Butler is far more successful as warden than her male predecessors, whose "throw away the key" attitude led to far more violence and danger than has been true since she became warden.[46]

Notes

1. Lois Higgins, "Historical Background of Police Women's Service," Journal of Criminal Law and Criminology, XLI, no.6 (March-April, 1951):822–825.

2. Ibid. 825.

3. Peter P. Horne, "The Role of Women in Law Enforcement," The Police Chief, vol. XL, no.7, (July 1973,):61.

4. Lois L. Higgins, Police Women's Manual, Springfield, IL: Charles C. Thomas, Inc., (1961):94.

5. Evabel Tenny, "Women's Work in Law Enforcement," Journal of Criminal Law, Criminology and Police Science, vol. XLIV, no.2 (August 1953):241.

6. Mary A. Anderson, Women in Law Enforcement: A Primer for Policewomen, (Portland, Metropolitan Press, 1973):9–30.

7. No author, "No longer men and women but police officers," U.S. News and World Report, vol. LXXVII, (August 19, 1974):46.

8. No author, "Federal Law Enforcement Goes Co-Ed," Women in Action, (June 1971):1–2.

9. Horne, "The Role of Women," etc.:67.

10. Gary R. Perlstein, "Police Women and Police Men: A Comparative Look," The Police Chief, vol. xxxix (March 3, 1972):74.

11. Gary R. Perlstein, "Certain Characteristics of Police Women," Police, XVI, no.5, (January 1972):46.

12. Stanley Martin, The Status of Women On the Move: The Status of Women in Policing, (Washington, DC: The Police Foundation):1990

13. Bureau of Labor Statistics, Employment (May 2014).

14. Peter Moskos, Cop in the Hood: My Year Policing Baltimore's Eastern District, Princeton, NJ: Princeton University Press, (2008):50–51.

15. Chris McNaughton, "Stress and Women Police", Women Police, vol.36, no.1 (Spring 2002):18.

16. Clayton Browne, "What Is a State Trooper?" Demand Media, http://woman.thenest.com/state-trooper-16981.html [accessed July 9, 2015].

17. Ibid.:3.

18. April Wickes, "Military Police Women: History in the Making," Joint Base Langley-Eustis, (March 25, 2013):1.

19. James J. Knights, "What Makes a Woman Valuable as an F.B.I. Special Agent?" Gender Watch, (September 2004):10–12.

20. Dorothy M. Schultz and Steven M. Houghton, "The Wisconsin Magazine of History, vol. 86, no.3, (Spring 2003):22.,

21. Ibid.:25.

22. National Center for Women and Policing, "Equity Denied: The Status of Women in Policing (Los Angeles, April 2002).

23. Jan McGregor, The Washington Post, (October 2, 2014):1.

24. No author, ""Policewoman: the first century and beyond," MCCC News (February 28, 2008).

25. Jess Siart, "Dobbs Ferry Police Chief Makes Her Mark," Daily Voice, (July 5, 2012):1.

26. Beth Pitts, "Penny Harrington, the USA's 1st Female Chief of Police," Business Magazine, (March 4, 2013):1.

27. Roland Smothers, "At Work With: Beverly Harvard; Atlanta's Police Chief Won More Than a Bet" The New York Times, (November 30, 1994):Home and Garden 1.

28. Isa Belkin, "Woman Named Police Chief of Houston," The New York Times, (January 20, 1990)::US1.

29. Ellis Stout, "Women in Probation and Parole," Crime and Delinquency, (January 1973):61—62.

30. No author, "Probation officer had 'affair' with convicted murderer," The Telegraph, (September 4, 2014):28.

31. U.S. Government, Department of Labor, Bureau of Labor Statistics, 2014.

32. 433 U.S. 321 See also: C. Cushman, Supreme Court Decisions and Women's Rights, (New York: CQ Press, 2001):122–128.

33. Cheryl Bowser Peterson, "Doing time with the boys," In: Barbara Raffel Price and Natalie Sokolof, eds. The Criminal Justice System and Women, New York: Clark Boardman Co. Ltd. (1982):437–462.

34. Ben M. Crouch and Geoffrey P. Alpert, "Sex and occupational socialization among prison guards: a longitudinal study," Criminal Justice and Behavior, vo. 9(1982):159–176.

35. Max Weber, The Theory of Social and Economic Organization, New York: Martino Fine Books (2012 org. 1947):26..

36. Ibid.:132.

37. James Terborg, "Socialization Experience of Women and Men," In: H.J. Bernardin. Ed. "Women in the Workforce, (New York: Prager, 1982).

38. Bob Egelko, "Female Guards Ok'd to Strip Search Male Inmates," San Francisco Gate, (May 21, 2009):1.

39. Carol Biemer, "The Role of the Female Mental Health Professional in a Male Correctional Setting," Journal of Sociology and Social Welfare, vol.4, (1977):882.

40. Alex Dominguez, "Tavon White, Inmate who impregnated four guards, guilty of racketeering, attempted murder. "The Huffington Post, (April 23, 2013):1.

41. No author, "Oregon inmate who had sex with two female guards sues for sexual harassment," Daily Mail, (May 9, 2015):1.

42. No author , "Female prison guard trainee charged with inmate sex in chapel," The Tribune Democrat, (January 24, 2014):1.

43. Josh Margolin and Meghan Keneally, "Joyce Mitchell arrested in Dannemora, N.Y. prison escape case,"ABC News Network, (June 12, 2015).

44. Tom Kane, "Prison has first female warden," The Daily Republican, (July 8, 2008):1.

45. David Middlecamp, "First Female Warden in Charge at California Men's Colony," San Luis Obispo Tribune, (May 2, 2010):Local News 1.

46. Valerie Schremp Hahn, "First female warden of maximum security Menard prison worked way up in system," St. Louis Post Dispatch, (May 28, 2014):News 1.

Chapter Eight

Women in Communications

I

When Nancy Dickerson became the first female correspondent for CBS, she entered an all male world. Prior to that momentous event, no woman had ever been seen on any TV news broadcast. The celebrities who dominated the news were Chet Huntley, David Brinkley, Walter Cronkite, Dan Rather, Doug Edwards, Bob Schieffer, and innumerable lesser lights who read the news in local TV stations from coast to coast.

Nancy Dickerson was a native of Wisconsin. She earned a degree in elementary education from the University of Wisconsin in 1948 and continued her education at the Catholic University in Washington, DC, where she studied speech and drama in an effort to enter a career in broadcasting. This led to her appointment in 1954 as the producer of Capitol Cloakroom, a radio show consisting of interviews with members of Congress. In 1960, she then advanced to become co-producer of Face the Nation, leading to her becoming the first female correspondent at CBS, the Columbia Broadcasting System. In 1963 she moved to NBC as a reporter. This gave her the opportunity to cover political conventions, election campaigns, and inaugurations, as well as Congress and the White House.[1]

In 1971, Nancy Dickerson became an independent producer, syndicating a daily news program called Inside Washington. She subsequently founded the Television Corporation of America, which produced documentaries, including "784 Days that Changed America-From Watergate to Resignation." For that she received the Peabody Award and the Silver Gavel from the American Bar Association.

In May 2008, Barbara Walters (Warmwasser) published her memoir after spending 46 years in television broadcasting, beginning in 1962 when she began work with Hugh Downs on the Today show. She continued in that position after Downs left and Frank McGee became the host. When McGee died in 1974, Walters was appointed co-host with Jim Hartz. Then, she worked with Harry Reasoner on ABC"s news program ABC Evening News as well as the ABC program 20/20, which employed her from 1979 to 2004.[2]

In the course of her long career, Walters interviewed almost every prominent politician available. She went to China with President Nixon in 1972 and interviewed the Prime Minister of Israel, Golda Meir, in 1973. In 1977 she interviewed the Prime Miinister of Israel, Menachem Begin, and the President of Egypt, Anwar Sadat, together. These examples are only a small portion of the work she did over so many years, as she worked for ABC News as reporter, author, and correspondent, and also hosted an interview program several times a year. She then created and co-hosted an interview program called The View. She retired from ABC News in 2014 with an estimated worth of $150 million.

Walters was married four times to three men. In 1955 she married Robert Henry Katz and divorced him in 1957. Lee Guber was her second husband, whom she married in 1963 and divorced in 1976. She adopted a child, Jacqueline, in 1968, and was married a third time in 1981 to Merv Adelson, whom she divorced in 1984 and remarried in 1986, only to divorce him again in 1992.[3]

Connie Chung, a lady of Chinese descent, became a co-anchor with Dan Rather at CBS in 1993. She left that assignment and produced her own show consisting of interviews with prominent people. When the female assistant to a congressman was murdered and suspicion centered on the congressman, Chung interviewed him. She also succeeded in gaining an interview with Klaus von Bulow, a prominent Danish immigrant and "playboy" who was acquitted of seeking to murder his wife. Connie Chung Tonight, her next hosting job, was cancelled after a short run. In 2003, Chung ended her brief television career after earning $4 million a year at ABC and $3 million a year at CNN.[4]

These women were the first to challenge the patriarchy which had been entrenched in the American communications industry for years. The consequences of this revolution were that in 2014 the Bureau of Labor Statistics reported that 59% of writers, 48% of editors, 44% of news analysts, and 25% of announcers were women, and that 73.6% of "miscellaneous" employees of the communications industry were also female.[5]

II

Melissa Francis exemplifies the success women have had in the television industry. A graduate in economics from Harvard University, she joined the Fox Business Network in January of 2012 as an anchor of MONEY with Melissa Francis as well as another program called Strange Inheritance Unpacked. Before joining Fox, Francis was an anchor at CNBC, where she hosted two programs as she became the first reporter to broadcast from the floor of the New York Mercantile Exchange. Earlier, Francis was correspondent for CNET broadcasts covering finance, technology, and consumer products. She began her career as anchor for a number of New England television stations in Hartford, Manchester, and Providence, and a researcher for the MacNeil-Lehrer News Hour. Melissa is married to Wray Thorn, with whom she has two children.[6]

Judy Woodruff and Gwen Ifill were named co-anchors of the first ever female co-anchor team to host the PBS NewsHour once hosted by Jim Lehrer, who retired. This was indeed a breakthrough development for both women, who testified that in their youth they never saw a woman on programs like News-Hour.[7]Judy Woodruff was crowned Young Miss Augusta in 1963 at age 17. She began her broadcasting career at ABC in 1970 in Atlanta , GA. and later moved to Washington, D.C. to work for NBC. Between 1972 and 1988 she covered the

White House as well as serving as Washington correspondent for the MacNeil-Lehrer NewsHour. She has been awarded the News and Documentary Emmy Award and the Cable ACE award.[8]

Vicky Newton was co-anchor for the weekday newscasts at KMOV-TB in St. Louis for ten years. She covered the news at 5 p.m., 6 p.m., and 10 p.m., and became the most popular news broadcaster in St. Louis until a stalker ruined her career. In her adolescence, she showed considerable talent playing the piano and considered a career in music. When she was still in high school, she was hired as a part time news reader on a local country music station. Later she attended Arkansas State University, earning a degree in journalism in 1997. She then worked in TV in Little Rock, Kansas City, and Detroit, where she did graduate work at the University of Detroit, followed by going to St. Louis in 2002. In 2003 she graduated with a master's degree in journalism. She was married for eight years bur then divorced, as her career led her to constantly move from city to city. Newton is one of the few Afro-Americans to succeed as an anchor. In 2008 she hosted a six months series on race relations in St. Louis. She won several awards including "Best TV Anchor" and "Woman of Achievement Award." She was a member of several boards of trustees associated with musical performances such as the St. Louis Symphony. She also played the piano at various benefits.[9]

After ten years Newton left KMOV in St. Louis because she was the victim of a "stalker" who sent her vast amounts of email each day, triggered her house alarm, and threatened her. She moved to Arkansas, her home state, where she resumed her TV career. The stalker was never apprehended.[10]

Susan Roesgen has been prime time news anchor for several TV stations since she began her career at CNN in 2005. In 2009 she moved to WGNO in New Orleans, the local ABC affiliate.

Roesgen is the daughter of William Roesgen, the editor of the Billings Gazette and former publisher of several newspapers. Her sister is a freelance television reporter. She graduated from Montana State University with an English literature major. This led to her first television job, writing commercials. Later she joined the news department as an anchor with WABC in New York City. Her reporting included Haiti and Israel and Egypt. She received an Emmy Award for a documentary and an Associated Press Award. Over the years Roesgen has worked for six TV stations, from Little Rock and New Orleans to San Diego, Chicago, Washington, and New York.[11]

Roesgen caused a considerable amount of criticism when she screamed at a participant in a government sponsored rally against federal spending and taxes because a participant criticized Barack Obama. Since she had previously become angry and abusive whenever someone disagreed with her "liberal" views, she was fired from her job at the Chicago based CNN in 2009. Subsequently she was appointed as an anchor at WGNO in New Orleans. There she hosts "News With a Twist," including taped conversations with a variety of guests.[12]

Sandra Gallant spent 15 years at WEEK-TV in Peoria, Illinois, where she broadcast the weather and also anchored the news. She also covered crime stories, including murder cases in central Illinois. In 2013 she covered a tornado hit in Peoria and in Washington, DC. She has repeatedly run the half-marathon and has engaged in weight training. A graduate of Florida State University, Gallant has also attended law school at Northern Illinois University. She was named as "The Best Meteorologist" before she left WEEK to spend time with her husband and two children. [13]

Virginia Kerr graduated from the University of Alabama in psychology. She began her broadcasting career on the production crew at WCTF in Tuscaloosa, Alabama. She was then appointed weekend anchor and general assignment reporter for KHO-TV in Spokane, Washington. Then she moved to Missoula, Montana as a morning anchor reporter, followed by becoming the evening anchor reporter. She joined KMOV-TV in St. Louis, MO, in 2003 as "Awake Anchor." There she was weekday feature reporter on "News 4 This Morning" for three years. Kerr is married and has one child. [14]

Karen Foss retired from KSDK-TV in St. Louis at the end of 2006. She had been anchorwoman for 27 years, since 1979. She won six Emmys, two for best anchor. She attained the highest "Q" rating as the best known news reader in the local market. In 2005 she was inducted in the Silver Circle by the National Academy of Television Arts and Sciences. The Press Club of St. Louis named her "Media Person of the Year." In addition she received eight more awards from a number of sources.Before she came to KSDK she began her television career at KCMO in Kansas City, MO. Foss was called "a pioneer for women" and "a leader in the news room for a quarter of a century." Over the years she reported on four presidential nominating conventions. Among other events, she reported on her trip to China. Foss was married four times. She has a daughter and is a grandmother. [15]

Pamela Silva Conde was born in Peru. She is a graduate of Florida International University where she earned a B.A. degree in broadcast journalism and a master's degree in business administration. She also earned a graduate certificate in bilingual education from St. Thomas University. Conde is a six time Emmy award winner and co-author of the Univision weekly newsmagazine First Impact, which broadcasts in Spanish. It is seen in the United States and in 12 Latin American countries. Her assignments lead her all over the U.S.A. and foreign countries.

Conde began her career at Univision in 2003 as public affairs coordinator for the community affairs show Miami Ahora on WLTV and worked for a network show called The Fat Man and the Skinny Woman. She then hosted a number of events for WAMI in Miami including News in 90, a 90 second summary of the news. She is also a cheerleader for the Miami Dolphins. In 2005, Conde joined the Univision of Miami news team as entertainment anchor and reporter. She was later named main anchor for the Spanish language morning newscast, where she presented the daily news. She also worked on special features and on investigative reporting.[16]

III

Women have made considerable contributions to journalism. This is in part true because so many women enroll in journalism schools. For example, in 2013 more than 75% of journalism students at American colleges were women. This was determined by the Annual Survey of Journalism and Mass Communication Enrollment. Female students had more success in the job market than male students because women specialized in public relations and advertising. One half had found a job by October 1 after graduating.[17]

Yet, the Women's Media Center reported that in 2014 women were credited with only 36.1% of total by lines as reporters or anchors. Even entertainment reporting, which is favored by women, exhibits a 61% to 39% majority for men. World politics, crime, and justice are far more likely to be covered by male reporters than by women. The New York Times has a very wide gender gap, with women credited with only 39% of published articles.[18]

The American University's Women and Politics Institute found that there are few women participating in Sunday morning talk shows. In fact, men have traditionally made up three quarters of the guests in these shows. This gender gap is attributed to widespread sexism in the media. Another reason for the lack of women in Sunday morning talk shows is that there are few women who possess political power, which is the reason men are asked to be guests on such shows. For example, only 16% of U.S. Senators are women, and women held only 16% of seats on important House committees. Therefore it is evident that the key to allowing more women to gain interviews on television is the election of women to public office.[19]

National Public Radio has a very positive record with regard to female employment. Three of five of its major shows are hosted by women. The CEO of NPR is a woman, as is the head of its news department. Yet, only 26% of people from outside NPR who were interviewed were female. Women make up 22% of the American radio workforce, but at NPR women are one half of the staff.[20]

A study of news programming on ABC, CBS, and NBC discovered that in 2007 men reported 48% and women 40% of news stories. The other twelve percent were reported by a team of men and women. In 1987, men reported 78% and women only 22% of news stories.[21]

There are some women who have attained outstanding achievements in journalism. One of these is Christiane Amanpour, the global affairs anchor for ABC news. She reports on major international events and anchors documentaries on international subjects. She is chief international correspondent for CNN. She covered the Gulf War and has reported from Iraq, Afghanistan, Iran, Pakistan, Israel, Rwanda, and the United States, and she has interviewed a large number of domestic and foreign politicians. Amanpour has received every major broadcast award and nine honorary degrees. She is also a member of the Excellent Order of the British Empire, as she was born in London and is a British citizen. She graduated from the University of Rhode Island with a B.S. in journalism.

Joan Didion was born in California. Her writing career began when she was a student of English at the University of California. She won an essay contest sponsored by Vogue Magazine, leading to a job in the New York office. She stayed there for two years while writing articles in a number of other magazines and publishing her first novel Run, River. That novel led to a contract to write another book. In 1963 she married John Dunne, who worked for Time Magazine. They moved to Los Angeles and adopted a baby girl. Didion and Donne both began to write in the "new journalism," consisting of writing in a personal style. She published Slouching Toward Bethlehem, a book dealing with the counterculture popular in the 1960's. Then Didion and Dunne together wrote the screenplay for the movie Panic in Needle Park, followed by a number of additional screenplays. Didion then wrote several essays and books dealing with South America. In 2003, both her husband and her only child died, leading to a book she wrote about her pain, The Year of Magical Thinking, which won The National Book Award in 2005. This was followed by Blue Nights in 2011. As a journalist, Didion is credited with articles which are viewed as standard texts in many schools of journalism.[22]

Nora Ephron was a journalist who also wrote plays, movie scripts, and books. She was born in 1941 in New York City. One of four sisters who also were screenwriters and novelists, Ephron was nominated three times for the Academy Award for best writing for When Harry Met Sally and Sleepless in Seattle. She also won a Drama Desk Award and a Tony Award for Lucky Guy. She also received the Women in Film Crystal Award.

She was married three times and had two sons. Ephron was a 1962 graduate of Wellesley College. After graduation she became a reporter for the New York Post for five years. She wrote a column on women's issues for Esquire and Cosmopolitan. She later also wrote for The Huffington Post. After her death in 2012, the Tribeca Film Festival established a "Nora Ephron Prize" for a female writer.[23]

Linda Greenhouse covered the Supreme Court for The New York Times for thirty years. She was awarded the Pulitzer Prize and other awards for her journalistic achievements. Like almost all journalists who seek recognition, she skewed her reports according to the so-called "liberal" position, which is best described as bias against the rights guaranteed American citizens by the first amendment to the U.S. Constitution. Greenhouse was born in New York City. She received a B.A. in government from Radcliffe College in 1968 and a law degree from Yale University in 1978. Greenhouse worked for the New York Times for forty years. She wrote over 2,800 articles for the Times and participated in the PBS Washington Week program. She retired from the New York Times in 2008.Greenhouse always inserted her private opinions into her reporting. She assaulted religion as well as any views not in consonance with her interpretation of women's rights or other "liberal" issues. She "second guessed " American foreign policy and defended terrorists imprisoned at Guantanamo Bay.[24]

Jane Kramer is a European correspondent for The New Yorker. She has written a "Letter from Europe" for twenty years. She has also written nine books, including Lone Patriot, which deals with the militia in the American West. Kramer was born in Rhode Island in 1938. She earned a B.A. in English from Vassar College and an M.A. in English from Columbia University. Her first journalism experience was at The Morningsider, followed by writing for The Village Voice. In 1981 she received the National Book Award for Nonfiction for The Last Cowboy. She has also received the Emmy Award for documentary filmmaking and the National Magazine Award, the Front Page Award, and the French "Prix européen de l'essai Charles Veillon" award. Kramer is a fellow of the American Academy of Arts and Sciences, a member of the Council of Foreign Relations, and a founding member of the Committee to Protect Journalists. She has taught at Princeton University, Sarah Lawrence College, SUNY, and the University of California at Berkeley. In 2006 she was elected to become a Chevalier de la Legion d'Honneur.[25]

Jane Mayer is an investigative journalist. She has been a staff writer for The New Yorker since 1995. Her most recent articles deal with the drone program, government prosecution of 'whistle blowers' and politics. Mayer was born in New York City in 1955. She is a descendant of Emanuel Lehman, one of the founders of the Lehman Brothers bank, and on her mother's side she descended from the historian Alan Nevis. In 1977 she graduated from Yale University, later studying at Oxford University.

Mayer began her career in Vermont writing for two small weekly papers. She later moved to The Rutland Herald, a daily paper. Then she became a reporter for The Washington Star and thereafter she joined The Wall Street Journal. During the 12 years she worked for The Wall Street Journal she reported from the White House, later becoming front page editor. She also served as foreign correspondent for The Journal, reporting on the bombing of the Marine barracks in Beirut, the Persian Gulf War, the destruction of the Berlin Wall, and the abolishing of communism in Russia. Mayer has written books dealing with Supreme Court Justice Clarence Thomas and with President Ronald Reagan.

Mayer married William Hamilton, a former editor of The Washington Post.Mayer wrote a number of articles about the influence of money in politics. She won the Toner Prize for Excellence in Political Reporting. Later she won a number of awards. She has also appeared on a number of television discussion shows.[26]

Mary McCarthy was called one of America's preeminent women of letters. She was therefore awarded the Edward McDowell Medal for outstanding contributions to literature. She wrote in an adversarial manner and attacked other female writers. This type of literary aggression was viewed as important warfare among the intellectual elites who pay attention to these writers, although only a small segment of the American population are aware that the McCarthys,, the Hellmans, or the Trillings exist. It is fairly evident that the literary opinion producers imagine themselves to be far more important than reality permits.

McCarthy wrote some novels which have been described as cultural history. These novels were almost entirely self-portraits. She wrote a memoir of her painful youth after her parents had died and she was raised by abusive relatives.

Mary Therese McCarthy was born in Seattle in 1912. Her father was a successful lawyer. Her parents died during the 1918 flu epidemic, so that she and her brothers were raised in Minneapolis by adults who beat them with razor straps and forced them to stand outside in the snow for hours. She was rescued by her maternal aunt, with whom she lived from the age of eleven. She attended Vassar College. She then engaged in a number of "love affairs" and divorced her first husband. She had one by her second marriage. She then devoted her life to writing, which included attacks on other writers. Her third husband was James West, with whom she lived in Paris and sometimes in Maine.

McCarthy wrote twenty-one books and an immense number of articles .[27]

Anna Quindlen was born in Drexel Hill, a suburb of Philadelphia, PA in 1952. As a reporter and columnist for The New York Times, Newsweek and The New York Post, she sought to provide a female perspective in the publications for which she wrote. Quindlen is a graduate of Barnard College. Quindlen began her career at the age of eighteen, when she became a copy girl. She worked for The New York Post as a reporter for four years, from 1974 to 1978, and then started at The New York Times as a reporter covering city hall. She also wrote a column "About New York" and "Living in the '30's." Her column "Public and Private" was published from 1990–1992 when she won a Pulitzer Prize. For Newsweek, Quindlen wrote a column called "Last Word." Her columns have been collected and published as books. Like all journalists who seek to succeed, Quindlen preached the "liberal" line, which consists of intolerance and name calling. She praised same sex marriage and attacked Rudy Giuliani, the former mayor of New York, and promoted women achievers in politics and in journalism. Quindlen also wrote about domestic violence. Some of her books were made into television movies, including three of her children's books. Anna Quindlen is chair of the Barnard College board of trustees. She holds three honorary doctorates, having promoted national abortion rights. Quindlen is married to Gerald Krovatin with whom she has three children.[28]

Gloria Steinem, a Presbyterian native of Toledo, Ohio, was born in 1934. Her mother was a newspaper employee and her father an antique dealer. Her grandmother, Pauline Steinem, was an activist in the women's suffrage movement. Her parents divorced when Gloria was eight years old. Thereafter she lived with her mother, who was emotionally ill. At age fifteen, Gloria moved to Washingon DC, where she lived with her sister. She entered Smith College at eighteen, graduating magna cum laude in 1956. She then lived in India for two years on a fellowship.

Steinem moved to New York in 1960, supporting herself by writing "free-lance" articles for various magazines and for a television show "That Was the Week that Was." She then investigated the working conditions of Playboy "bun-nies." To do so, she became a "bunny" herself. After three weeks she quit and wrote an article exposing the poor working conditions ad substandard wages women received for working long hours in demeaning circumstances as rich men enjoyed the 'atmosphere." In 1968, Steinem co-founded New York maga-zine and became an editor and writer of "leftist" articles. She supported Demo-crats for various offices and lent support to the United Farm Workers. She then became involved in the women's liberation movement and agitated for legal abortion. In the 1960's she worked for the civil rights movement and the move-ment against the Vietnam War. Her most important role, however, was to act on behalf of women. She joined Bella Abzug and Betty Friedan to form the Nation-al Women's Political Caucus and fought for an abortion plank in the Democrat platform during the presidential election convention of 1972. That year also, she founded MS., a women's action magazine which attained a circulation of 500,000 in five years. In 1983, she published a book including her experiences working tirelessly for gender equality.[29]

Dorothy Thompson was an American journalist who was expelled from Na-zi Germany in 1934. In 1939, Time magazine called her one of the two most influential women in America. Eleanor Roosevelt was the other one. She wrote a column carried by 170 newspapers and was read by eight to ten million people each day.

Dorothy Thompson was born in 1893 of a British father and an American mother. When she was only eight years old, her mother died. She moved to Chi-cago when her father remarried. She graduated from Syracuse University and then moved to Buffalo, NY where she became active in the suffragette move-ment. She then moved to Europe and, as a freelancer, sold her articles to various magazines. This led her to become the Philadelphia Public Ledger bureau chief in Berlin. In 1931 she interviewed Adolf Hitler before Hitler became dictator. She made some hostile remarks concerning Hitler, and was therefore expelled from Germany in 1934. She came back home and warned her country of the danger of Nazism. She also delivered a number of radio addresses in which she tried to help the refugees from Nazi Europe. Her column was called "On the Record," in which she supported Republican candidates for political office until she switched parties in the midst of the 1940 presidential campaign and sudden-ly supported Roosevelt. This led Republican newspapers to drop her column. She also agitated against Jews in a most vociferous manner, which led the New

York Post to drop her column. This was particularly surprising as she had married a Hungarian Jew while in Europe. She divorced Josef Bard after she returned to New York, and then married the novelist Sinclair Lewis, with whom she had a son, Michael Lewis. In 1942 she divorced Sinclair Lewis and married a third time. Her third husband was Maxim Kopf, with whom she stayed until her death in 1960.[30]

IV

There can be little doubt that Jacqueline Bouvier Kennedy Onassis was the most famous American woman book editor in her own day and today. Her fame as former First Lady and wife of President Jack Kennedy made her the target of endless news articles and comments in all the media. Therefore, her entrance into editing after the death of her second husband received considerable publicity. Mrs. Onassis was not a newcomer to the communications industry. She had graduated from George Washington University in 1951 with a degree in literature, and thereafter worked for The Washington Times Herald as an "Inquiring Photographer." After her second husband died she returned to New York, and subsequently became an editor for the Viking Press when she was 46 years old. After three years at Viking she moved to Doubleday. Her name was a great asset to the publishing companies she served. This led the publishers to hand her assignments, which made her most productive. Jackie Bouvier Kennedy Onassis died of cancer in 1994.[31]

According to "The Bureau of Labor Statistic,s" editors earn an average annual salary of $53,880. That is indeed a low income if compared to other industries. It is nevertheless not surprising, as the entire communications business is low paying and poorly rewarded, except for a few "superstars."

Ellen Archer is President of Hyperion, a subsidiary of Disney-ABC Group. She joined Hyperion in 1999 as Vice President and Associate Publisher. In 2001, she was promoted to Vice President and Publisher and in 2005 she became Senior Vice President. During her tenure at Hyperion she was responsible for numerous best selling campaigns, including "The Five People You Meet in Heaven" by Mitch Albom, a popular sportswriter. She also published "Trading Up" and "Lipstick Jungle" by Candace Bushnell, and "The Tender Bar" by J. Moehringer. These books are mainly of interest to middle aged women. Before working for Disney, Archer was Vice President and Associate Publisher of Ballantine, a division of Random House. She succeeded in a number of marketing campaigns for numerous titles commonly sold to readers with limited education. Earlier she was Vice President at Doubleday. Archer is a board member of NYU's "Masters in Publishing" program. She holds a bachelor's degree in English from Hamilton College.[32]

Anna Wintour is undoubtedly the most successful female editor in the United States. Born in England to a privileged family, she is the descendant of numerous British nobles. She is the editor of Vogue, an American fashion magazine located in New York City. Her annual income is estimated at $2 million. Wintour is the daughter of Charles Wintour, editor of the Evening Standard. From him she learned a great deal about journalism. She moved to New York and worked briefly for House and Garden and later for New York.

Wintour took fashion classes in London at the behest of her parents. She became an editorial assistant at Harper's Bazaar, beginning her career in fashion journalism. By associating with numerous influential older men, she succeeded in becoming fashion editor at Viva, a women's magazine. Later she became fashion editor for Savvy in New York and from there became fashion editor at New York. In 1983 Wintour was appointed to work at Vogue, editing the British magazine. She returned to New York and worked briefly for House and Garden, until in 1987 she became editor of the American Vogue. Her career in that position has been made into a movie, "The Devil Wear Prada," starring Meryl Streep. "Her leadership of that magazine led to her being named "Editor of the Year" and also led to her appointment to the honorary title of "Officer of the Order of the British Empire" conferred by Queen Elizabeth II. Subsequently, Wintour was honored and featured in numerous other situations which seem remote from the lives of the vast majority of Americans, who have no interest in fashion and seldom, if ever, encounter that bizarre world known almost only to the rich and the super-rich.[33]

Pamela Geller is the editor of Atlas Shrugs, a magazine devoted to the support of free speech and the freedom of the press in the spirit of John Peter Zenger, who defied the British governor in 1733, and Thomas Jefferson, the third President of the United States, who furnished the Constitution with the First Amendment. Geller is also the president of the American Freedom Defense Initiative, which seeks to maintain freedom of speech in this country. Geller is the author of The Post-American Presidency, and a regular columnist for World Net Daily, the American Thinker, and other publications. She has been the recipient of numerous honors such as the Guardian of Freedom Award, and was honored as the "American Patriot of the Year" in 2013. In addition to numerous other recognitions, the U.S. Marine Corps presented her with the flag flown on September 11, 2001 over Camp Leatherneck. Geller is a frequent contributor to numerous newspapers and often appears as a guest on TV and radio shows. Geller has opposed the Islamization of the United States.[34]

Katrina vanden Heuvel has been the editor, publisher and part-owner of The Nation magazine since 1995. A frequent guest on television programs, she discusses politics and foreign relations. Her mother, Jean Stein, is the editor of Grand Street, a literary journal, and her father, William, is a former ambassador, author, and member of the Kennedy Administration. Her grandfather, Jules Stein, founded the Music Corporation of America.

Katrina graduated from the Trinity School and then studied politics and history at Princeton University. Then she became the editor of Nassau Weekly, graduating summa cum laude in 1981. During her tine at Princeton she worked part time for The Nation. She became part owner of The Nation by investing in it. That led to her becoming editor-at –large in 1989 and editor in 1995. She also became a columnist for The Washington Post. She is a frequent commentator on a number of nationally televised discussion programs concerned with politics and international affairs. She is the recipient of numerous awards and supports various Arab organizations.

Vanden Heuvel is married to Steven Cohen, a professor at Princeton University, with whom she has one child.[35]

There are many more women working in communications than could be presented here, In fact, there is an Association of Women in Communications with 2,500 members in all fifty states.

Notes

1. John Dickerson, On Her Trail: My Mother, Nancy Dickerson, (New York: Simon and Schuster, 2006):153.

2. Barbara Walters, Audition: A Memoir, (New York: Alfred A. Knopf, 2008):7–13.

3. Ibid:262–269.

4. Bill Carter, "CNN Cancels her Program and Chung Quits Network," The New York Times, (March 26, 2003):B1.

5. Bureau of Labor Statistics, Table 11 (2014).

6. Micki Siegel, "Sseet Melissa," New York Post, November 22, 2012):1.

7. Katherine Fung, "Judy Woodruff and Gwen Ifill named PBS Co-Anchors," The Huffington Post, (August 6, 2013).

8. No author, "Judy Woodruff plans to leave CNN in June," The New York Times, (April 29, 2005):1.

9. Eileen P. Duggan, "Vicky Newton: Fantasy to be TV anchor came true," St. Louis Journalism Review, (December 2008):1.

10. Laurelei Livingston, "Vickie Newton: Stalker Pursues News Talker," Tight Entertainment, (December 29, 2012):1.

11. K. Daniel Glover, "Ex-CNN Star: Roesgen Crossed a Journalistic Line," Accuracy in Media, (April 21, 209):1.

12. Ibid:1.

13. http://dodoodad.com/sandy-gallant-biography/ [accessed June 11, 2015].

14. http://www.zoominfo.com//p/Virginia-Kerr/178274664 [accessed June 11, 2015].

15. http://www.prnewswire.com/news-releases/ameren-corporation-directors-elect-highly-respected-st-louis-newscaster-karen-foss-vice-president-public-relations-58043872.html [accessed June 11, 2015].

16. Susmita Barat, "Pamela Silva Conde, Univision anchor, To Become Next 'The View' Host? Latin Times, (May 31, 2013):1.

17. Sheila Gibbons, "Industry Statistics," Media Report to Women, (March 12, 2012).

18. Antara Sinha, "Gender gaps in journalism classes and newsrooms concern students," USA Today, (February 17, 2015):1.

19. Gail Baitinger, "Why are there so few women on the Sunday morning talk shows?" The Washington Post, (January 8, 2015):1.

20. Jesse Ellison, "How NPR Became a Hotbed for Female Journalists," Newsweek, (March 5, 2012).

21. Kathleen Ryan , "Gender split in broadcast news reporting," Electronic News, vol.4, no.10, (February 2010):1.

22. Joan Didion Biography - Academy of Achievements(April 2, 2012).

23. Adam Bernstein, "Nora Ephron, prolific author and screenwriter," The Washington Post, (June 26, 2012).

24. Tony Mauro, "A Goodbye for Greenhouse," Legal Times, (June 12, 2008):1.

25. Robert S. Boynton, "Jane Kramer," The New Journalism, (March 11, 2012):1.

26. "Jane Mayer," The Writers Directory, (Detroit:St. James Press. June 10, 2011).

27. "Mary McCarthy", The New York Times, (October 29, 1029):Books 1.

28. Anna Quindlen, (March 13, 2005), http://www.annaquindlen.com [accessed June 11, 2015].

29. "Gloria Steinem," Encyclopedia of World Biography, 2004.

30. "Dorothy Thompson," Dictionary of American Biography, 2007.

31. Jocelyn Noveck, "Jackie O's Other Life: As Book Editor," The Huffington Post, (December 17, 2010):1.

32. No author, "Elle Arcer", Bloomberg Business Week, (May, 29, 2015):1.

33. Cathy Horyn, "Citizen Anna," The New York Times, (February 1, 2007):Fashion 1.

34. Anne Barnard and Alan Feuer, "Pamela Geller - Provocateur, Lightning Rod," The New York Times, (October 10, 2010):New York Region:1.

35. No author, "Katrina vanden Heuvel," Farmington Hills,, MI, Contemporary Authors, Thomson Gale(2005):422–425.

Postscript

Social change is permanent and inevitable. In some centuries it is so slow that it appears that nothing ever changed. This was true during the years sometimes called "The Dark Ages."

The changes which brought about women's ascendancy in the United States are related to a great number of movements in American society which were not seen as having anything to do with women's liberation, but nevertheless resulted in that great gender revolution which is the subject of this book.

When the sewing machine was invented, it relieved women of a terrible task which seemed never to end, as they slaved over the repair and construction of clothes for their families every day. Then the refrigerator relieved women of the need to cook anew or preserve food under primitive conditions.

These inventions, and many others, were accompanied by an increase in longevity, allowing both genders more time to go to school and to escape the drudgery of farming. In fact, in 1920 all states demanded that girls and boys attend school, so that for the first time girls were allowed a free education.

When the Afro-American population demanded the right to vote and to be free of racial discrimination, women followed and demanded the same for themselves. This came about in the 1960's, as electronics reduced muscle work and increased "white collar" work, so that women could now earn money and declare their independence from a man's paycheck.

All of this led to an increase in women's self-image, allowing women to run for public office and promoting their interests with vigor and confidence.

Therefore it is the thesis of this book that within another generation the United States will become a feminist society governed by women and led by the "weaker sex" in all the institutions reviewed here.

BIBLIOGRAPHY

BOOKS

Anderson, Mary A., *Women in Law Enforcement: A Primer for Policewomen*, (Portland: Metropolitan Press, 1973)

Baltzell, E. Digby, *The Protestant Establishment*, (New York: Random House, 1964)

Blair-Loy, Mary, *Competing Devotions*, (Cambridge, MA: Harvard University Press, 2003)

Bonin, John and Louis Putterman, *Economics of Cooperation and the Labour Managed Economy*, (London: Routledge, 2001)

Braiker, Henry, *The Type E Woman: How to Overcome the Stress of Being Everything to Everybody*, (Lincoln, NB: iUniverse, Inc., 2006)

Burckel, Nickolas C., "Oberlin College," *Handbook of American Women's History*, (Thousand Oaks, CA: Sage Publications, 2000)

Burns, Nancy, Kay L. Schlossman and Sidney Verba, *The Private Roots of Gender Action*, (Cambridge: Harvard University Press, 2001)

Campion, Nardi, *Ann the Word: The Life of Mother Ann Lee, Founder of the Shakers* (Boston: Little Brown, 1976)

Carroll, Susan J. and Kira Sanbonmatsu, *Entering the Mayor's Office: Women's Decisions to Run for Municipal Office*, (Chicago: The Midwest Political Science Association, 2010)

Castro, Ginette, *American Feminism*, (Paris, France: National Political Science Press)

Center for American Women and Politics, *Women Mayors in U.S. Cities 2014*, (New Brunswick, NJ: Eagelton Institute of Politics, 2014)

Clinton, Hillary Rodham, *Hard Choices*, (New York: Simon and Schuster, 2014)

———, *Living History*, (New York: Simon and Schuster, 2003)

Courtwright, David T., *No Right Turn: Conservative Politics in a Liberal America*, (Cambridge, MA: Harvard University Press, 2010)

Cushman, C., *Supreme Court Decisions and Women's Rights*, (New York: CQ Press, 2001)

de Bary, William Theodore, Jerry Kisslinger, and Tom Mathewson, eds., *Living Legacies at Columbia*, (New York: Columbia University Press, 2006)

Delli Carpini, Michael X. and Scott Keeter, *What Americans Know About Politics*, (New Haven: Yale University Press, 1996)

Dickerson, John, *On Her Trail: My Mother, Nancy Dickerson*, (New York: Simon and Schuster, 2006)

Encyclopedia of World Biography: 2007 Supplement (Farmington Hills, MI: Gale, 2007)

Encyclopedia of World Biography: 2004 Supplement (Farmington Hills, MI: Gale, 2004)

Federoff, Nina, "Barbara McClintock," *Biographical Memoirs, vol.* 68 (Washington, DC: The National Academy Press, 1995)

Fisher, Bonnie S., Francis T. Cullen and Michael G. Turner, *The Sexual Victimization of College Women*, (St. Paul, MN: Minnesota Center against Violence and Abuse, 2000)

Francis, Richard, Ann the Word: *The Story of Ann Lee* (New York: Arcade Publishing Co., 2000)

Friedan, Betty, *The Feminine Mystique*, (New York: W.W. Norton & Co., 1963)

Greeley, Andrew M., *Angry Catholic Women*, (Chicago: Thomas More Press, 1985)

Greene, Meg, *Sonia Sotomayor: A Biography*, (New York: Greenwood Publishers, 2012)

Gutmann, Stephanie, *Kinder, Gentler Military*, (New York: Scribner, 1997)

Harris, Alice Kessler, *Bread Givers*, (New York: George Braziller, 1975)

Haveman, Robert and Barbara Wolfe, *Where Are the Asset Poor?* (Madison, WI: Robert M. La Follette School of Public Affairs, 2000)

Hawthorne, Robert, Jr., "Freda Porter Locklear," *American Indian Biographies*, Harvey Markovitz, Editor, (Ipswich, MA: Salem Press, 1999)

Higgins, Lois L., *Police Women's Manual*, (Springfield, IL: Charles C. Thomas, Inc., (1961)

Hollis, Ernest V. and Alice A. Taylor, *Social Work Education in the United States*, (New York: Columbia University Press, 1951)

Holm, Jeanne, *Women in the Military*, (Novato, CA: Presidio Press, 1992)

Horowitz, Helen L., *Alma Mater: Design and Experience in the Women's Colleges*, (Amherst: University of Massachusetts Press, 1993)

Howe, Irving, *World of Our Fathers*, (New York: Harcourt, Brace, Jovanovich, 1976)

Jacobson, G.C., *Politics of Congressional Elections*, (New York: Pearson, 2012)

James, Edward T., Janet James and Paul Boyer, *Notable American Women: A Biographical Dictionary*, (Cambridge, MA: Harvard University Press, 1971)

Keller, Rosemary, Rosemary Radford Ruether and Marie Canton, *Encyclopedia of Women and Religion*, (Indianapolis, IN: Indiana University Press, 2006)

Klingsbury, Nancy and John Scanzoni, "Structural Functionalism," In: *Sourcebook of Family Theories*, William J. Doherty, Editor (New York: Plenum Press, 1993)

La Beau, Dennis, Editor, *Theater, Film and Television Biographies*, (Detroit: Gale Research Co. Index Series, 2013)

League of Women Voters, *History of the League of Women Voters*, (Washington DC, 2011)

Lindley, Susan Hill, *You Have Stepped Out of Your Place*, (Louisville, KY: Westminster John Knox Press, 1996)

Lofas, Jeanette, *Step-Parenting*. (New York: Kensington Publishing Co., 2004)

Maddox, Brenda, *Rosalind Franklin: The Dark Lady of DNA*, (New York: Harper Collins, Publishers, 2002)

Maraniss, David, *First in His Class: A Biography of Bill Clinton*, (New York: Touchstone Press, 1995)

Margolis, Max L. and Alexander Marx, *A History of the Jewish People*, (Philadelphia: The Jewish Publication Society, 1960)

Martin, Susan E., *Women on the Move? A Report on the Status of Women in Policing*, (Washington, DC: The Police Foundation, 1990)

Mayer, Susan T., *What Money Can't Buy: Family Income and Children's Life Chances*. (Cambridge, MA: Harvard University Press, 1997)

Miller, Mary, *The Brave Women of the Gulf Wars*, (New York: 21st Century Publishers, 2006)

Moskos, Charles C. and John Sibley Butler, *All That We Can Be: Black Leadership and Racial Integration the Army Way*. (New York: Basic Books, 1996)

Moskos, Peter, *Cop in the Hood: My Year Policing Baltimore's Eastern District*, (Princeton, NJ: Princeton University Press, 2008)

No author, "Blackwell, Antoinette Louise Brown," in *The National Encyclopedia of American Biography*, vol. 19 (New York: James T. White & Co., 1941)

No author, "Katrina vanden Heuvel," *Contemporary Authors*, (Farmington Hills,, MI: Thomson Gale (2005)

Oliver, Melvin L. and Thomas M. Shapiro, *Black Wealth, White Wealth: A New Perspective on Racial Inequality*, (New York: Routledge, 1995)

Peterson, Cheryl Bowser, "Doing time with the boys," In: Barbara Raffel, Price and Natalie Sokolof, eds. *The Criminal Justice System and Women*, (New York: Clark Boardman . Ltd., 1982)

Potucheck, John L., *Who Supports the Family?* (Stanford, CA: Stanford University Press, 1997)

Rhodes, Richard, *Hedy's Folly: The Life and Breakthrough Inventions of Hedy Lamarr*, (New York: Doubleday, 2012)

Ricks, Thomas E., *Making the Corps*, (New York: Simon and Schuster, 1997)

Safra, Jaqui, "Linda B. Buck," *Encyclopedia Britannica*, (Chicago, IL: Merriam-Webster, 2004)

Sanbonmatsu, Kira, Susan B. Carroll, and Debbi Walsh, *Poised to Run: Women's Pathway to the State Legislatures*, (New Brunswick, NJ: Rutgers: The State University of New Jersey, 2009)

Shannon, Jacqueline, *Dream Doll: The Ruth Handler Story*, (Stamford, CT: Longmeadow Press, 1995)

Siegvold, Paul, *The Ideal American Lady*, (New York: Putnam's, 1893)

Skraine, Rosemary, *Women in Combat*, (Santa Barbara, CA: ABC-CIO, 2011)

Slater, Robert and Elaine Slater, *Great Jewish Women*, (Middle Village, NY: Jonathan David, Publisher, 2004)

Smith, Marjorie Proctor, "Who do you say I am? Mother Lee as Christ," *Locating the Shakers*, (Exeter, England: University of Exeter Press, 1990)

Sobel, Robert, *Biographical Directory of the Governors of the United States, vol.4*, (Westport, CT: Meckler Books, 1978)

Terborg, James, "Socialization Experience of Women and Men," In: H.J. Bernardin. Ed., "Women in the Workforce, (New York: Prager, 1982)

Thomas, William I., *The Child in America: Behavioral Problems and Programs*, (New York: Knopf, 1928)

Tobin, Jeffrey, *The Nine: Inside the Secret World of the Supreme Court*, (New York: Doubleday, 2007)

Treadwell, Mattie E., *The Women's Army Corps*, (Washington DC: Office of the Chief of Military History, 1954)

Underhill, Andrew F., *Valued Observations to So-called Christian Science*, (Yonkers, NY: Arlington Chemical, 1902)

Vatican Congregation for the Doctrine of the Faith, "Declaration on the Question of the Admission of Women to the Priesthood," in Rosemary Radford Ruether, Ed., *Women-Church: Theology and Practice* (San Francisco: Harper & Row, 1986)

Walters, Barbara, *Audition: A Memoir*, (New York: Alfred A. Knopf, 2008)

Weber, Max, *The Theory of Social and Economic Organization*, New York: Martino Fine Books (2012, org. 1947)

Williams, Selma R., *Divine Rebel: The Life of Ann Marbury Hutchinson*, (New York: Holt, Rinehart and Winston, 1981)

Woodmansee, Laura, *Women Astronauts*, (Burlington, ON: Apogee Books, 2002)

Writers Directory, The, (Detroit: St. James Press. 2011)

Zeiger, Susan, *In Uncle Sam's Service: Women Workers with the American Expedition-ary Force, 1910–1919*, (Ithaca: Cornell University Press, 1999)

DOCUMENTS

19th Amendment to the Constitution of the United States

433 U.S. 321

ADEA Survey of American Dental School Applicants, (American Dental School Association: 2010)

Air Force Personnel Center, "Air Force Military Demographics"

American Physical Society, "Women in Physics", (2014)

American Academy of Physician Assistants, National Physician's Assistants Study: Census Report, (Washington DC, 2013)

Beede, David, et.al. '"Women in STEM," U.S. Department of Commerce, (2009)

Biographical Directory of the U.S. Congress, Debra Fischer, (Washington DC: The United States Government Printing Office, 2013)

Biographical Directory of the United States Congress, (C.Q. Staff Directories, 2004)

Bond, James T., Ellen Galinsky and Jennifer E. Swanberg, "The National Study of the Changing Workforce, New York, (Families and Work Institute, 1998)

Bramlett, Matthew, et.al., Cohabitation, Marriage, Divorce and Remarriage in the United States, vol.22, no.2 (U.S. National Center for Health Statistics, 2002)

Bureau of Labor Statistics, Current Population Survey, "Median Weekly Earnings of Full time Wage and Salary Workers by Detailed Occupation and Sex," Annual Average (2013)

Bureau of Labor Statistics, Employed Persons by Occupation, Sex and Race, (2013)

———, Employment (May 2014)

———, Labor Force Statistics from the Current Population Survey (2013)

Burelli, Daniel F., "Women in Combat: Issues for Congress," Washington DC: Congressional Research Service, (May 9, 2013)

Center for American Women and Politics, (New Brusnswick: Rutgers, The State University of New Jersey) Fact Sheet, No date.

Constitution of the United States, Amendment XXIII.

Curtis, John W. and Saranna Thornton, "Here's the News: The annual report on the economic status of the profession," University Faculty, (March-April 2013)

Dempsey, Martin, "Allowing women in Combat Strengthens Joint Force," American Forces Press Service, (January 24, 2013)

Department of Defense, "Women in the Military," (12/27/13)

Freedom House, Freedom in the World, 2013.

Gibbons, Sheila, "Industry Statistics," Media Report to Women, (March 12, 2012)

National Association of Women Lawyers, Report of the Sixth Annual National Survey on Retention and Promotion of Women in Law Firms, (October 2011)

National Center for Educational Statistics, "Digest of Education Statistics, (2011)

———, Digest of Educational Statistics, (2013)

National Center for Women and Policing, "Equity Denied: The Status of Women in Policing (Los Angeles, April 2002)

No author, "2014 Ivy League Admission Statistics," The Ivy Coach, (2014)

No author, "Ellen Ochoa," National Aeronautic and Space Administration, (Houston,Texas, 2013)

No author, "Tomorrow's Doctors: Tomorrow's Cures," Washington, DC: Association of American Medical Colleges, (2013)

No author, A Current Glance at Women in the Law, Chicago: The American Bar Association, (2013)

No author, Centers for Disease Control, "National Intimate Partner and and Sexual Violence Survey," (November 2011)

No author, Women in STEM: a Gender Gap to Innovation. U.S. Department of Commerce, Economics and Statistics Administration, (August 2011)

Office of the Under Secretary of Defense, Personnel and Readiness, "Report to Congress on the Review of Laws Policies and Regulations Restricting the Service of Female Members in the U.S. Armed Forces, (2012)

Pew Research Center Analysis of the Decennial Census and American Community Surveys

Report on Interservice Academy Conference, (October 20, 1975)

Robinson, B.A., "Ontario Consultants on Religious Tolerance," July 15, 2011.

Robinson, Bruce R., "When Churches Started to Ordain Women," Ontario Consultants on Religious Tolerance, (March 29, 2011)

Schmelzer, Ranit, "High School Dropouts: a Problem for Girls and Boys, Answer Bag," (Washington, DC: National Women's Law Center, October 30, 2007)

U.S. Bureau of Labor Statistics, 2013, Annual Social and Economic Supplements to the Current Population Survey.

U.S. Bureau of the Census, "Percentage of People 25 Years Old and Over Who Have Completed High School or College," (June 24, 2004)

———, (2011) Percentage of Managers in the Private Sector Who Are Female, 1970–2010 (2011)

———, Statistical Abstract of the United States, 2011. (Washington, D.C. U.S. Government Printing Office. Table 600)

U.S. Catholic Demographic Census

U.S. Department of Agriculture. Expenditure on Children by Families, (Washington, DC, 2013)

U.S. Department of Commerce, Bureau of the Census, (Washington, DC: United States Government Printing Office, 2013)

U.S. Department of Education, National Center for Educational Statistics, (2013)

U.S. Department of Labor, Bureau of Labor Statistics, Employed Persons by Sex, Race and Ethnicity, (2013)

U.S. Department of Labor, Bureau of the Census, "Households by type and tenure of householder," (2013)

United States Department of Labor. Bureau of Labor Statistics. "America's Young Adults at 27," (March 26, 2014.)

White, Susan, et. al. "Female Students in High School Physics," (College Park, MD: American Institute of Physics, 2011)

Wickes, April. "Military Police Women: History in the Making," Joint Base Langley-Eustis, (March 25, 2013)

Wolff, Edward N. "Recent Trends in the Size and Distribution of Household Wealth," (Working Paper No. 300), Annandale-on-Hudson, NY: Jerome Levy Economics Institute of Bard College

JOURNAL ARTICLES

Abrahams, N., ""Negotiating Power, Identity, Family and Community," *Gender and Society*, vol.10, no.6, (1996)

Bainbridge, William S., "Shaker Communities," *Journal for the Scientific Study of Religion*, vol. 49, no. 1, (2010)

Barnett, Rosalind and J.B. James, "The psychological effects of work experiences and disagreements about gender role beliefs in dual earner couples," *Women's Health: Research on Gender, Behavior and Policy*. Vol.4, (1998)

Bertrand, Marianne, et.al. "Dynamics of the gender gap for young professionals in the financial and corporate sectors, " *American Economics Journal: Applied Economics*, vol. 2, (2010)

Beutel, Ann M. and Margaret M. Marini, "Gender and Values," *American Sociological Review*, vol.60, (1995)

Bey, D.R. and J. Lange, "Wailing Wives: Women Under Stress," *American Journal of Psychiatry*, V. 131, (1974)

Biemer, Carol, "The Role of the Female Mental Health Professional in a Male Correctional Setting," *Journal of Sociology and Social Welfare*, vol.4, (1977)

Bowen, G.I., "Spouse support and the retention intentions of Air Force members," *Evaluation and Program Planning*, vol. 9, (1986)

Bower, Bruce, "The Dating Go Round," *Science News*, (February 14, 2009)

Brett, Jeanne and Linda K. Stroh, "Working 61 plus hours a week. Why do managers do it? " *Journal of Applied Psychology*, vol.86, (2003)

Bumpass, Larry L. and Hsien-Hen Lu, "Trends in Co-habitation and Implication for Children," *Population Studies*, vo,54, (2000)

Burtless, Gary, "Growing American Inequality: Sources and Remedies," *The Brookings Review*, vol. 17, no.1

Cawley, James T., et.al. "Physician Assistants in American Medicine," *The American Journal of Managed Care*, vol.19, no.10, (2013)

Cherlin, Andrew J., "American Marriage in the 21st Century," *Future Child*, Fall 2005.

Cohen, Jere, "Parents as educational models and definers," *Journal of Marriage and the Family*, 49(2)

Cohen, Lisa, Joseph P. Broschak and Heather A. Haveman, "And Then There Were More? *American Sociological Review* vol.36, (1998)

Cohen, Steven M., "American Jewish Feminism: A Study in Conflict and Compromises," *American Behavioral Scientist*, vol. 23, no. 4, (1980)

Cook, Elizabeth and Clyde Wilcox, "Feminism and the Gender Gap," *Journal of Politics*, vol. 53, (1991)

Cooper, Ralph A., "Impact of trends in primary, secondary and post-secondary education on applicants to medical school," *Academic Medicine*, vol.78, no.9, (2003)

Crane, Frank, "Christian Science and Insanity," *Methodist Review*, vol. 91 (May 1909)

Crouch, Ben M. and Geoffrey P. Alpert, "Sex and occupational socialization among prison guards: a longitudinal study," *Criminal Justice and Behavior*, vol. 9(1982)

Davies, Paul G., Stephen J. Spencer and Claude M. Steele, "Clearing the Air," *Journal of Personality and Social Psychology*, vol.88, (2005)

Dwek, Carol, et. al., "Sex Differences in Learned Helplessness," *Developmental Psychology*, vol. 15 (1978)

Ebaugh, Helen and Paul Ritterband, "Education and the Exodus from Convents," *Sociological Analysis*, vol. 39, (1978)

Elder, Laurel, "Contrasting Party Dynamics" *Social Science Journal*, vol.51, No.3, (September 2014)

Fenster, J.M., "The Woman Who Invented the Dishwasher," *Inventions and Technology*, (February, 1999)

Finkel, Eli and Paul Eastwick, "Speed Dating," *Current Direction in Psychological Science*, vol.17, no.3 (June 2008)

Fox, Margery, "Protest in Piety: Christian Science Revisted," *International Journal of Women's Studies*, vol. 1 (July –August 1978)

Freeman, Jonathan, Eric Heiman, Collen M. Carpinella, Kerri L. Johnson, Jordan B. Leitner, "Early Processing of Gender Cues Predicts the Electoral Success of Female Politicians," *Social Psychological and Personality Science*, vol. 5, no.7 (September 2014)

Halperin, John, "Trollope and Feminism," *South Atlantic Quarterly*, vol. 77 (Spring 1978)

Hamilton, Brady E. et. al. "Annual Summary of Vital Statistics, 2011," *Pediatrics*, vol. 131, no.3 (February 11, 2013)

Harris, Alice Kesller, "Organizing the Unorganizable: The Jewish Women and their Union," *Labor History*, (Winter 1976)

Heckert, Alex and Thomas C. Nowak, "The Impact of husbands and wives relative earnings on marital disruption," *Journal of Marriage and the Family*, vol. 60, (1998)

Heilman, Madeline E., "Description and Prescription: How Gender Stereotypes Prevent Women's Ascent up the Organizational Ladder," *Journal of Social Issues*, vol. 57, (2001)

Higgins, Lois, "Historical Background of Police Women's Service," *Journal of Criminal Law and Criminology*, XLI, no.6 (March-April, 1951)

Hill, David B., "Political Culture and Female Political Representation," *Journal of Politics*, vol. 43, (1981)

Horne, Peter P., "The Role of Women in Law Enforcement," *The Police Chief*, vol. XL, no.7, (July 1973,)

Kaplan, Mordecai, "What the American Jewish Woman Can Do for Adult Jewish Education," *Jewish Education*, vol. 4 (October-December 1932)

Kaufman, Dorothy, "Women Who Return to Orthodox Judaism," *Journal of Marriage and the Family*, vol. 47, (1985)

Kelley, M.L. et. al. "Effects of military induced separation on the parenting stress and family functioning of deploying mothers," *Military Psychology*, vol. 6 (1994)

Khonou, Grace, "Social Work is Women's Work," *The Social Work Practitioner*, vol. 24, no.1, (2012)

Knapik, J.J., K.I. Reynolds and F. Herman, "Soldier load carriage: Historical, physiological, biomechanical and medical aspects," *Military Medicine*, vol.169, no.1, (2004)

Kohut, Rebecca, "Jewish Women's Organizations in the United States," *American Jewish Yearbook*, 1930–1932, (Philadelphia: Jewish Publication Society, 1931), vol. 33:175

Lareau, Annette and Elliott Weininger, "Time, Work and Family Life," *Sociological Forum*, vol.23, (2008)

Lat, David, "How Did the Law School Class Of 2013 Do In The Job Market?" *Above the Law*, (June 20, 2014)

Lege, David and Thomas A. Trozzolo, "Who Participates in Local Church Communities?" *Origins*, V. 15, 1985

Lerner, Ann Lapidus, "Who Has Not Made Me a Woman: The Movement for Equal Rights for Women in American Jewry," *American Jewish Yearbook*, (1977)

Marini, Stephen, "A New View of Mother Ann Lee and the Rise of American Shakerism," *Shaker Quarterly*, vol. 18, (1990)

Marshall, Ann, "Organizing Across the Divide," Social Science Quarterly, vol.83 (2002)

McDowell, Sarah, "Research reveals a gender gap in the nation's biology labs," *PhysOrg*, June 30, 2012

McNaughton, Chris, "Stress and Women Police", *Women Police*, vol. 36, no.1 (Spring 2002)

Mobius, J.P., "The Physiological Mental Weakness of Women and the Lower Races," *Alienist and Neurologist*, vol. 22 (October 1901)

Nash, Margaret and Lisa Romero, "Citizenship for the College Girl," *Teacher's College Record*, vol. 114. No. 2 (2012)

Neal, Maria Augusta, "Women in Religious Symbolism and Organization," *Sociological Inquiry*, vol. 49 (1979)

Nguyen, Hannah-Hanh D. and Marie Ryan, "Does stereotype threat affect test performance of minorities and women?" *Journal of Applied Psychology*, vol. 93, (2008)

No author, "Federal Law Enforcement Goes Co-Ed," *Women in Action*, (June 1971)

No author, "The Nurse's Contribution to American Victory," *American Journal of Nursing*, vol. 45, (September 1945)

No author, "Wage Gap Persists for Women Physicians-Researchers," *Journal of the American Medical Association*, (June 15, 2012)

No author, "Women and the Military," *Minerva Quarterly*, (Spring 1988)

Nursing Council on National Defense, *American Journal of Nursing*, vol.40, (September 1940)

Origins (May 2, 1985)

Palmer, Bruce, and David Simon, "The Political Glass Ceiling: Gender, Strategy and Incumbency," *Women and Politics*, vol. 23, no2, (2001)

Pandorf, C. et.al. "Correlates of load carriage and obstacle course performance among women," *Work*, vol.18, no.2, (2002)

Parsons, Jacquelynne E., "Cognitive Developmental Factors in Emerging Sex Differences in Achievement Related Expectancies," *Journal of Social Issues*, vol. 32, (1976)

Perlstein, Gary R., "Certain Characteristics of Police Women," *Police*, XVI, no.5, (January 1972)

———, "Police Women and Police Men: A Comparative Look," *The Police Chief*, vol. xxxix (March 3, 1972)

Petri, Lucille, "The U.S. Cadet Nurse Corps: A Summing Up," *American Journal of Nursing*, vol.45, (1945)

Powers, Elizabeth T., "Does means testing welfare discourage savings?" *Journal of Public Economics*, vol. 68, (1998)

Rice, T. and D.L. Coates, "Gender Role Attitudes in the Southern United States," *Gender and Society*, vol. 9, no.6, (1995)

Riddle, Larry, "Karen E. Smith," *The Notices of the American Mathematical Society*, vol.48, no.4, (April 2001)

Rossi, Mary Ann, "Priesthood, Precedent and Prejudice," *Journal of Feminist Studies in Religion*, vol. 7, no. 1, (Spring 1991)

Rury, John, "Vocationalism for Home and Work: Women's Education in the United States, 1880–1930," *History of Education Quarterly*, vol. 24, no.1, (1984)

Salee, Shelley, "The Woman of It: Governor Miriam Ferguson's 1924 Election," *Southwestern Historical Quarterly*, vol. 100, (July 1996)

Schneider, Dorothy and Carl J. Schneider, "Transition to the Military," *Educational Horizons*, vol. 64, No. 3 (Spring 1966)

Stark, Rodney, "The Rise and Fall of Christian Science," *Journal of Contemporary Religion*, vol. 12, no. 2 (1998)

Stout, Ellis, "Women in Probation and Parole," *Crime and Delinquency*, (January 1973)

Tenny, Evabel, "Women's Work in Law Enforcement," *Journal of Criminal Law, Criminology and Police Science*, vol. XLIV, no.2 (August 1953)

Tomlinson, Everett T., "The Decline of the Ministry," *World's Work, New York*, vol. 8 (December 1904)

Treas, Judith and Eric D. Widmer, "Married women's employment over the life course," *Social Forces*, vol.78, (2000)

Wegland, Glendyne, "Our Shaker Ancestors," *New England Ancestors*, vol. 7, no. 0–6, (2006)

Welch, Susan and Albert K. Karnig, "Correlates of female office holding in city politics," *Journal of Politics*, vol. 41, (1979)

Wilcox, Clyde, "The causes and consequences of feminist consciousness," *Comparative Political Studies*, vol. 23, (1991)

Wolfers, Justin, "Diagnosing Discrimination," *Journal of the European Economic Association*, vol.4, no.3, (April-May 2006)

Wynd, C.A. and Dziedzicki, R.E. "Heightened anxiety in Army reserve nurses anticipating mobilization during Operation Desert Storm," *Military Medicine*, vol. 157, (1992)

Zenko, Micah and Amelia MacWolf, "Our Military, Our Selves," *Foreign Policy*, (May 21, 2013)

Zweifler, Seth, "University of California gets an unexpected leader in Janet Napolitano," *The Chronicle of Higher Education*, (July 18, 2013)

NEWSPAPERS, MAGAZINES, & BROADCASTS

Anderson, Nick, "The Gender Factor in College Admissions, *The Washington Post*, (March 26, 2014)

Baitinger, Gail, "Why are there so few women on the Sunday morning talk shows?" *The Washington Post*, (January 8, 2015)

Barat, Susmita, "Pamela Silva Conde, Univision anchor, To Become Next 'The View' Host? Latin Times, " (May 31, 2013)

Barkhorn, Eleanor, "Getting Married Later Is Great for College-Educated Women," *The Atlantic*, (March 15, 2013)

Barnard, Anne and Alan Feuer, "Pamela Geller - Provocateur, Lightning Rod," *The New York Times*, (October 10, 2010):New York Region

Belkin, Isa,"Woman Named Police Chief of Houston," *The New York Times*, (January 20, 1990)

Bernstein, Adam, "Nora Ephron, prolific author and screenwriter," *The Washington Post*, (June 26, 2012)

Boorstein, Michelle, "Reclaiming the Feminine Spirit in the Catholic Priesthood," *The Washington Post*, (July 30, 2006)

Borlik, Alicia K., "DoD Marks 50th year of Military Women's Integration," *DoD News*, (June 17 1998)

Boynton, Robert S., "Jane Kramer," *The New Journalism*, (March 11, 2012)

Brown, Eric, "What's Next for Jill Abramson's 'T' Tattoo?" *International Business Times*, (May14, 2014)

Brown, Hayes, "Armed Forces Sexual Assault Crisis Reaches New Heights," *Think Progress*, (May 15, 2013)

Bumiller, Elisabeth and Thom Shanker, "Pentagon Is Set to Lift Combat Ban for Women," *The New York Times*, (January 23, 2013)

Burns, Hilary, "There are 100 women in Congress for the first time in history," *Business First*, (November 5, 2014)

Cahillane, Kevin, "The Women of West Point", *The New York Times Magazine* (September 4, 2014)

Carlson, Nicholas, "The Truth About Marissa Mayer," *Business Insider*, (August 25, 2013)

Carter, Bill, "CNN Cancels her Program and Chung Quits Network," *The New York Times*, (March 26, 2003)

Chen, Pauline W., "Sharing the Pain of Women in Medicine," *The New York Times*, (November 29, 2012)

Conti, Allie, "The State of the Aging Sisters," *Vice*, (July 22, 2013)

Drew, Christopher, "Where the Women Are," *The New York Times*, (April 4, 2011)

Duggan, Eileen P., "Vicky Newton: Fantasy to be TV anchor came true," *St. Louis Journalism Review*, (December 2008)

Egelko, Bob, "Female Guards Ok'd to Strip Search Male Inmates," *San Francisco Gate*, (May 21, 2009)

Ellison, Jesse, "How NPR Became a Hotbed for Female Journalists," *Newsweek*, (March 5, 2012)

Foster, George, "Women Bad for Cadet Morale?" *Air Force Times*, (May 22, 1974)

Fung, Katherine "Judy Woodruff and Gwen Ifill named PBS Co-Anchors," *The Huffington Post*, (August 6, 2013)

Glover, K. Daniel, "Ex-CNN Star: Roesgen Crossed a Journalistic Line," *Accuracy in Media*, (April 21, 209)

Goldman. Ann, "The Papal Visit: Nun Still Keeps the Faith On Larger Women's Role," *The New York Times*, (September 18, 1987)

Goldman, Ari L., "Go-Ahead for Altar Girls," *The New York Times*, (July 2, 1994)

Gose, Ben, "Red Cross Appoints New CEO", *The Chronicle of Philanthropy*, (April 8, 2008)

Greenbaum, Julie, "Glass Ceiling Twice Shattered at Board of Rabbis," *The Jewish Journal of Greater Los Angeles*, (May 6, 2009)

Greenfield, Daniel, "Welfare State Watch: 40% of Babies born to Unmarried Mothers." *Front Page Magazine*, (August 28, 2012)

Hahn, Valerie Schremp, "First female warden of maximum security Menard prison worked way up in system," *St. Louis Post Dispatch*, (May 28, 2014)

Horyn, Cathy, "Citizen Anna," *The New York Times*, (February 1, 2007)

Hymowitz, Carol and Sarah Frier, "IBM's Rometty Breaks Ground as Company's First Female Leader," *Bloomberg Business Week*, (October 26, 2011)

Jaffe, Matthew "Boys and Girls Club CEO Roxanne Spillett's $1M Total Compensation Under Fire," *ABC News*, (March 12, 2010)

Kane, Tom, "Prison has first female warden," *The Daily Republican*, (July 8, 2008)

Katz, Raye T., "Exploring the Link Between Womanhood and the Rabbinate," *Lilith*, vol. 14, (1980–1986)

Kaufman, David, "Introducing America's First Black Female Rabbi," *Time*, (June 6, 2009)

Kenney, Jack, "Wanted: Women in Combat for Wars Without End," *New American*, December 22, 2014)

Klahr, Renee, "College Magazine's Top Ten Journalism Schools," *College Magazine*, (March 12, 2012)

Knights, James J., "What Makes a Woman Valuable as an F.B.I. Special Agent?" *Gender Watch*, (September 2004)

Lamothe, Dan, "Adm. Michelle Howard becomes First Four Star Woman in Navy History," *The Washington Post*, (July 1, 2014)

Liberto, Jennifer, "New peek into Caroline Kennedy's Wealth," *Money*, (August 19, 2013)

Livingston, Laurelei, "Vickie Newton: Stalker Pursues News Talker," *Tight Entertainment*, (December 29, 2012)

Mansfield, Harvey S., "Why a woman can't be more like a man," *The Wall Street Journal*, November 3, 1997)

"Mary McCarthy", *The New York Times*, (October 29, 1029):Books 1.

Margolin, Josh and Meghan Keneally, "Joyce Mitchell arrested in Dannemora, N.Y. prison escape case," *ABC News Network*, (June 12, 2015)

Martinez, Luis, "Air Force's Sexual Assault Prevention Officer Charged With Sexual Battery," *World New*, (May 6, 2013)

Mauro, Tony, "A Goodbye for Greenhouse," *Legal Times*, (June 12, 2008)

McClory, Robert, "Pope Francis and Women's Ordination," *National Catholic Reporter*, (September 16, 2013)

McGregor, Jan, *The Washington Post*, (October 2, 2014)

McMurran, Kristin, "Reagan is Shortchanging Women, Says GOP Feminist Kathy Wilson," *People*, vol. 20, no. 5, (August 1, 1983)

Middlecamp, David, "First Female Warden in Charge at California Men's Colony," *San Luis Obispo Tribune*, (May 2, 2010)

Mohler, Albert, "Virtual Adultery-The Emergence of Cyber Sinning," *The Sydney Morning Herald*, (August 22, 2005)

National American Women's Suffrage Association, "Resolution adopted at the annual convention," *Women's Citizen*, (April 5, 1919)

Newton-Small, Jay and Zeke J. Miller, "Talent at the Top," *Time*, vol. 184, no. 20 (November 24, 2014)

No author, "20/50: The Esquire Survey of American Men," *Esquire Magazine*, vol. 17, no.1 (October, 2013)

No author, "Female prison guard trainee charged with inmate sex in chapel," *The Trib-une Democrat*, (January 24, 2014)

No author, "Balancing Work and family: Four Women Executives Speak," *Leadership*, (May 24, 2000)

No author, "Capt. Kathleen McGrath, Pioneering Warship Commander," *The New York Times*, (October 1, 2002)

No author, "Drew Faust," *Boston Business Journal*, (May 19, 2014)

No author, "Elena Kagan: Associate Justice, Supreme Court," *The Wall Street Journal*, (August 4, 2014)

No author, "Elle Arcer," *Bloomberg Business Week*, (May, 29, 2015)

No author, "First Enlisted Women are Sworn In by Navy," *The New York Times*, (July 8, 1948)

No author, "Gail Collins," *The New York Times* (July 18, 2007)

No author, "House Ok's Girl Cadets," *Gazette Telegraph*, (June 30, 1975)

No author, "Irene Blecker Rosenfeld Is the CEO of Kraft Foods, Inc." *The Telegraph*, (June 10, 2014)

No author, "Judy Woodruff plans to leave CNN in June," *The New York Times*, (April 29, 2005)

No author, "No longer men and women but police officers," *U.S. News and World Report*, vol. LXXVII, (August 19, 1974)

No author, "Oregon inmate who had sex with two female guards sues for sexual harassment," *Daily Mail*, (May 9, 2015)

No author, "Our War Heroes," *Chicago Tribune*, (September 24, 2006)

No author, "Policewoman: the first century and beyond," *MCCC News*, (February 28, 2008)

No author, "Posthumous honor for fallen Air Force 1st Lt.," *Jewish Lights*, (January 29, 2010)

No author, "Probation officer had 'affair' with convicted murderer," *The Telegraph*, (September 4, 2014)

No author, "Sandra Day O'Connor," *Bio. A&E Television Network*, 2014

No author, "Top 10 Women's College Majors," *Forbes*, (March 2, 2010)

No author, "Woman Episcopal Priest Celebrates Communion," *The New York Times*, (January 3, 1977)

Peters, Mark and David Wessel, "More Men in Prime Working age Don't Have Jobs," *The Wall Street Journal*, (February 6, 2014)

Pitts, Beth, "Penny Harrington, the USA's 1st Female Chief of Police," *Business Magazine*, (March 4, 2013)

Pitts, Jonathan, "Right at Home," *The Baltimore Sun*, (March 9, 2008)

Purdy, Adoratia, "Dunwoody Relinquishes Command of Army Material Command," *Army Magazine*, (August 7, 2012)

Rampless, Catherine, "U.S. Women on the Rise as Family Breadwinners," *The New York Times*, (March 29, 2013)

Religious News Service, "First Female Southern Baptist Preacher Dies," (December 17, 2005)

Roberts, Sam, "For Young Earners in Big City, Gap Shifts in Women's Favor," *The New York Times*, (August 3, 2007)

Schafer, Susan M., "S.C. Gov. Haley's Husband Deploys with Guard," *Army Times*, (January 10, 2013)

Schmitt, Eric,"First Woman in 6 Decades Gets the Army's Silver Star," *The New York Times*, (June 17, 2005)

Schultz, Dorothy M. and Steven M. Houghton, *The Wisconsin Magazine of History*, vol. 86, no.3, (Spring 2003)

Siart, Jess, "Dobbs Ferry Police Chief Makes Her Mark," *Daily Voice*, (July 5, 2012)

Siegel, Deborah, "The New Trophy Wife," *Psychology Today*, (January 1, 2004)

Siegel, Micki, "Sweet Melissa," *New York Post*, November 22, 2012)

Sinha, Antara, "Gender gaps in journalism classes and newsrooms concern students," *USA Today*, (February 17, 2015)

Smothers, Roland, "At Work With: Beverly Harvard; Atlanta's Police Chief Won More Than a Bet," *The New York Times*, (November 30, 1994)

Stamberg, Susan, "Female WWII Pilots: The Original Fly Girls," *Morning Edition, NPR*, (March 9, 2010).

Stephanie Coontz, "How Can We Help Men? By Helping Women" *The New York Times*, (January 11, 2014)

Stewart, James B., "A CEO's Support System," *The New York Times*, (November 5, 2011)

Stolberg, Sheryl and Melissa Heay, "Harassment is Old Battle for Many Army Women," *Los Angeles Times*, (November 15, 1996)

Sweet, Lynn, "Pritzker appointed Secretary of Commerce," *Chicago Sun-Times*, (May 2, 2013)

Thompson, Mark, "Female Generals: The Pentagon's First Pair of Four Star Women," *Time Magazine*, (August 13,2012)

Thompson, Mark, "The Rise and Fall of a Female Captain Bligh," *Time*, (March 3, 2010)

Trevizo, Perla, "Women overtake men in earning degrees at all levels," *Time Free Press*, (February 21,2012)

Turbett, Peggy, "Case Western Reserve university president, Barbara Ann Snyder, is well compensated," *The Cleveland Plain Dealer*, (December 16, 20+13)

Tyson, Ann Scott "The Expanding Role of G.I. Jane," *The Christian Science Monitor*, (April 3, 2008)

Vlasic, Bill, "New G.M. Chief Is Company Woman, Born To It," *The New York Times*, (December 12, 2013)

Whitman, Rusty, "NM Direct Taps Turney as President, Chief Exec," *Women's Wear Daily*, vol 177, no. 54

Williams, Alex, "The End of Courtship," *The New York Times*, (January 30, 2013)

Woodhouse, Kelli, *Ann Arbor News*. (May 16, 2014)

"Your World with Neil Cavuto," *FOX News* TV Broadcast. January 4, 2008.

WEBSITES

Biesecker, Michael, "Rapid Fall for Army General Accused of Sex Crimes," Associated Press, (January 6, 2014)

Biographical Directory of the United States Congress. "Kay Bailey Hutchinson," (Washington DC: U.S. Government Printing Office, 2005)

Browne, Clayton, "What Is a State Trooper?" Demand Media, http://woman.thenest.com/state-trooper-16981.html [accessed July 9, 2015]

Burns, Robert, "Army Sexual Assault Prevention Office Coordinator Accused of "Abusive Sexual Contact," Huffington Post, (May 14, 2013)

Catalyst: "Catalyst Quck Take: Women in Law in the United States," (New York: Catalyst, 2013)

College of Arts and Sciences, American University: "Physics Courses," http://www.american.edu/cas/physics/courses.cfm, accessed April 30, 2015

deVise, Daniel, "More Women Than Men Got PhDs Last Year," http://www.washingtonpost.com/wp-dyn/content/article/2010/09/13/AR2010091306555.html, accessed April 30, 2015

Dominguez, Alex, "Tavon White, Inmate who impregnated four guards, guilty of racketeering, attempted murder. "The Huffington Post, (April 23, 2013)

The Family Research Council, (http://www.frc.org), accessed May 11, 2015

Grove, Allen, "Bryn Mawr College," Top Women's Colleges in the United States, http://collegeapps.about.com/od/collegeprofiles/p/BrynMawr.htm [accessed April 30, 2015]

Harvard Law School, "2010–2015 Course and Schedule Updates", http://hls.harvard.edu/dept/academics/curriculum/course-and-schedule-updates/ [accessed April 30, 2015]

Higher Education & Ministry, http://www.gbhem.org/clergy/clergywomen/history, (accessed April 24, 2015)

http://biology.case.edu/undergraduate/bachelor-of-arts-biology [accessed April 30, 2015]

http://chem.virginia.edu/undergraduate-studies-/chemistry-maj [accessed April 30, 2015]

http://dodoodad.com/sandy-gallant-biography/ [accessed June 11, 2015]

http://elementaryeducation.buffalostate.edu/childhood-education-grades-0–0–bs-0, accessed April 30, 2015

http://louisville.edu/dentistry/degrees/dmd/curriculum/first-year [accessed April 30, 2015]

http://www.biography.com/people/meg-whitman-20692533 "Meg Whitman," [Accessed May 12, 2015]

http://www.bloomberg.com/research/stocks/people/person.asp ?personId=7785847&ticker=1137:HK (accessed April 14, 2015)

http://www.nwpc.org./history

http://www.politico.com/magazine/story/2015/01/senate-women-secret-history-113908_Page2.html#.VWSK-tHbKEU (accessed May 26, 2015)

http://www.prnewswire.com/news-releases/ameren-corporation-directors-elect-highly-respected-st-louis-newscaster-karen-foss-vice-president-public-relations-58043872.html [accessed June 11, 2015]

http://www.zoominfo.com//p/Virginia-Kerr/178274664 [accessed June 11, 2015]

https://catalog.ufl.edu/ugrad/current/journalism/majors/journalism.aspx, [accessed April 30, 2015]

Hubbard, Ralph G., "The Second Term Economy," The Wall Street Journal, (November 17, 2004)

Joan Didion Biography - Academy of Achievements (April 2, 2012)

"Katherine Ann Couric," The Biography .com Website, http://www.biography.com/people/katie-couric-9542060, accessed April 30, 2015

Kirby, Brandon, "Pamela Silva Conde", Hollywood Reporter, (September 20, 2012), hollywoodreporter.com

Kirkwood, R. Cort, "The Military vs. Free Speech," https://www.lewrockwell.com/2003/06/r-cort-kirkwood/the-military-vs-free-speech/ (June 21, 2003), [accessed June 3, 2015]

Lasser, Carol, "Blackwell, Antoinette Louisa Brown," American National Biography Online, http://www.anb.org/articles/15/10–00064.html, accessed April 21, 2015

Laughlin, Sean and Robert Yoon, "Millionaires Populate U.S. Senate," All Politics, (June 13, 2003)

Liedtke, Michael, "Hewlett-Packard CEO Meg Whitman Gets Raise from $1 to $1.5 Million," Huffington Post, (December 17, 2013), http://www.huffingtonpost.com/2013/12/17/hp-raises-ceo-whitmans-s_n_4462281.html [accessed June 26, 2015]

No author, "Biograph: Donna Byrd," History Makers, (January 31, 2014), http://www.thehistorymakers.com/biography/donna-byrd

No author, "Birthrate in the United States 2013 by education attainment of mother 24519/statistics. www.statista.com

No author, "Contributions of 20th Century Women to Physics," Washington DC, The American Physical Society, http://cwp.library.ucla.edu, accessed April 30, 2015

No author, "Rev. Antoinette Brown seems to have made a failure of her first pastorate," Boston Investigator, (May 6, 1857), 19th Century US Newspapers via Gale Group, http://infotrac.galegroup.com

No author, "Ten Things You Didn't Know About Women Owned Businesses" http://mashable.com/2012/08/14/facts-women-business (accessed April 14, 2015)

Noveck, Jocelyn, "Jackie O's Other Life: As Book Editor," The Huffington Post, (December 17, 2010)

Quindlen, Anna, (March 13, 2005), http://www.annaquindlen.com [accessed June 11, 2015]

Rasmussen Report, "54% Favor Full Combat Role for Women in Military," http://www.rasmussenreports.com/public_content/politics/general_politics/febr uary_2012/54_favor_full_combat_role_for_women_in_military (accessed June 3, 2015)

Riddle, Larry, "Nancy Reid," Biographies of Women Mathematicians, (Decatur, GA, 2013). http://www.agnesscott.edu/lriddle/women/reid.htm [accessed July 9, 2015].

Ryan, Kathleen, "Gender split in broadcast news reporting," Electronic News, vol.4, no.10, (February 2010)

University of Buffalo School of Medicine and Biological Sciences, MD Degree Curriculum. http://medicine.buffalo.edu/education/md/curriculum.html, accessed April 30, 2015

University of Cincinnati, Family Nurse Practioner Curriculum," http://nursingonline.uc.edu/online-nursing-degree/nursing-specialties/family-nurse-practitioner/, accessed April 30, 2015

Women's Media Center, http://www.shesource.org/experts/profile/evelyn-murphy, (accessed May 12, 2015)

INDEX